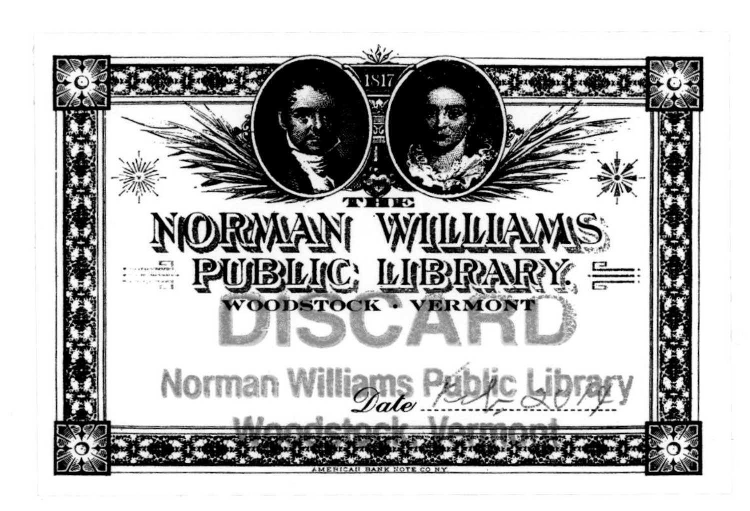

WEEKENDS FOR TWO IN NEW ENGLAND

BY BILL GLEESON | PHOTOGRAPHS BY CARY HAZLEGROVE

weekends for two IN NEW ENGLAND

SECOND EDITION • COMPLETELY REVISED AND UPDATED

50 ROMANTIC GETAWAYS

CHRONICLE BOOKS
SAN FRANCISCO

Library of Congress Cataloging-in-Publication Data available.

ISBN-10: 0-8118-4623-7
ISBN-13: 978-0-8118-4623-3

Manufactured in China

Designed and typeset by Deborah Bowman

Distributed in Canada by Raincoast Books
9050 Shaughnessy Street
Vancouver, British Columbia V6P 6E5

10 9 8 7 6 5 4 3 2 1

Chronicle Books LLC
85 Second Street
San Francisco, California 94105

www.chroniclebooks.com

ACKNOWLEDGMENTS

The author wishes to thank Yvonne Gleeson for research assistance and project coordination. The photographer wishes to thank Sarah Hazlegrove and Virginia Bullington.

Table of Contents

Introduction

Whoever coined the adage "Home is where the heart is" neglected to mention that home is also where the jobs, errands, children, telephones, and pots and pans are. Let's face it: there are times when the heart, at least the romantic part, needs a change of scene. And because romantic respites from parenting, dual careers, cooking, and cleaning come all too infrequently, choosing a suitably romantic destination is probably the most important decision you'll make when planning a cherished weekend away.

Unfortunately, our choices are often a blind leap of faith, based largely on recommendations from well-meaning friends, self-serving brochures that stretch the definitions of romantic and charming, or guidebooks created by writers who never ventured beyond the lobby.

The idea for a discerning, dependable series of romantic travel guides was conceived after one too many unpleasant weekends in unappealing lodgings inaccurately portrayed by innkeepers and friends as "romantic." Armed with specific criteria and a critical eye, we hit the road with the goal of separating travel fact from fiction.

SELECTION

Our process of identifying New England's most romantic inns and small hotels wasn't completely scientific. We considered recommendations from well-seasoned travel professionals whose opinions we respect, and then we conducted our own personal inn-to-inn searches along thousands of miles of highways and byways in six states: Maine, Vermont, New Hampshire, Massachusetts, Connecticut, and Rhode Island.

In narrowing our list to fifty, consideration was given to providing our readers with a range of accommodations in terms of rates, sizes, locations, ambience, and settings.

ROOMS FOR ROMANCE

When evaluating the romantic appeal of a property, we consider the following criteria, honed through visits to destinations around the country. We look for:

- Private bathrooms (a must in our opinion)
- In-room fireplaces
- Tubs or showers designed for two
- Breakfast in bed
- Down comforters
- Canopied, four-poster, and king-sized beds
- Couches, love seats, or nooks for sitting together
- Private decks, patios, or balconies with inspirational views
- Romantic décor and special touches such as fresh flowers and music
- Rooms where smoking is never permitted

We also seek out small hotels and inns that exude the overall, sometimes difficult-to-describe intimate atmosphere that engenders romantic sparks. And while we've nothing against children (we have two of our own), we have come to appreciate policies that discourage younger visitors. Many couples are seeking a well-deserved break from the kids, and the (sometimes loud) evidence of little people in the room next door or in the hall doesn't exactly contribute to a passionate getaway.

Finally, we avoid destinations referred to in the lodging industry as homestays. These are houses in which a room or rooms are rented out to travelers, often by resident owners lacking skill in the art of innkeeping.

Within the inns and small hotels listed in this book, we discovered special rooms that are particularly conducive to a romantic experience. Instead of leaving the choice of rooms to the reservation clerk and describing in detail the public areas of each establishment, we've devoted a good part of this book to details of particularly romantic rooms and suites. When booking your getaway reservation, don't hesitate to ask about the availability of a specific room.

TABLES FOR TWO

At the beginning of each regional listing, we've identified particularly noteworthy restaurants near our featured destinations. These were sampled by us and/or recommended by innkeepers whose opinions we respect. Keep in mind, however, that restaurants—and chefs—come and go. Accordingly, we suggest you balance these recommendations with updates and new choices offered by your innkeeper, who will be happy to offer suggestions.

YOUR FAVORITES

If we've overlooked one of your cherished destinations, please let us know by visiting www.billgleeson.com or by writing to us in care of Chronicle Books, 85 Second Street, San Francisco, CA 94105. We look forward to sharing new romantic weekends for two in future printings.

ABOUT RATES

Travelers scouting New England's highways for discount lodgings can still find a no-frills motel room for $50, but this guide isn't for bargain hunters. We view our romantic times together as the most special occasions, and through years of travel we've confirmed that you really do get what you pay for. Consequently, you should understand that a special room usually commands a higher price. In fact, you'll find few rooms described in these pages for less than $100 per night.

Many of our featured destinations offer substantially reduced rates during midseason and low-season, which vary widely by location. Also, keep in mind that most of our recommended properties require two-night minimum stays during weekends and holidays.

To help you plan your getaway budget, approximate high-season weekend nightly rates for specific rooms are noted within each description. Rates (per night for two friendly people) are classified at the end of each listing in the following ranges, not including tax:

Moderate: Under $200
Expensive: $200 – $300
Deluxe: Over $300

FINAL NOTES

No payment was sought or accepted from any establishment in exchange for a listing in this book.

Food, wine, and flowers were occasionally added to our photo scenes for styling purposes. Some inns provide these amenities; others do not. Please ask when making a reservation whether these items are complimentary or whether they're provided at an extra charge.

Please note that many interiors may have changed since photography was taken for our first edition. Please check inn Web sites for the most up-to-date photos. Also, we cannot guarantee that these properties will maintain furnishings or standards as they existed on our visit, and we very much appreciate hearing from readers if their experience is at variance with our descriptions. Reader comments are carefully consulted in the creation and revision of each Weekends for Two volume. Please visit www.billgleeson.com for updates and to provide feedback. Your opinions are important to us.

DAYTIME DIVERSIONS

Acadia National Park, one of New England's crown jewels, offers BAR HARBOR–area visitors some two hundred miles of hiking trails and "carriage paths," as well as freshwater lakes and beaches for swimming. Early-morning visitors to the summit of Cadillac Mountain are the first in the continental United States to see the sunrise.

The Pilgrim's Inn will provide you with a box lunch for an excursion by boat to charming ISLE AU HAUT. Works by the more than seventy members of the Maine Crafts Association are sold at the organization's shop in DEER ISLE.

A ferry departs several times daily from near the Inn at Sunrise Point to the island of ISLEBORO, where well-heeled New Englanders escape to impressive summer homes.

In KENNEBUNKPORT, you can escape the crowded village streets to romantic Parsons Beach, just southwest of town, or stroll the peaceful gardens of St. Anthony's Franciscan Monastery off Beach Street in a quiet corner of the lower village.

Rather than joining the busy weekend traffic that winds along Ocean Avenue around Cape Arundel and past the Bush family compound on Walker's Point, we recommend parking your car (weather permitting, of course) and strolling along the seaside walk.

TABLES FOR TWO

A number of inns described in this section have their own dining rooms. Our innkeepers also recommend:

PIER 77, Kennebunkport
CAPE ARUNDEL INN, Kennebunkport
WHITE BARN INN, Kennebunkport
MAGGIE'S CLASSIC SCALES, Bar Harbor
GAYLEN'S RESTAURANT AND GALLEY LOUNGE, Bar Harbor
PORTS OF ITALY, Boothbay Harbor
LOBSTERMAN'S WHARF, East Boothbay

MAINE

THE FACTS

Eighteen rooms, each with private bath. Complimentary full breakfast served at tables for two in dining room. No disabled access. Smoking is not permitted. No minimum stay requirement. Closed from mid-November through mid-April. Moderate to expensive.

GETTING THERE

From Maine Turnpike (Interstate 95) at Bangor, take Route 395 bypass to Route 1A and follow to Ellsworth (Route 1A becomes Route 3). Follow Route 3 into Bar Harbor. Turn left on West Street and follow to inn on right.

Manor House Inn
106 West Street
Bar Harbor, ME 04609
Telephone: (207) 288-3759;
toll-free: (800) 437-0088
Web site: www.barharbormanorhouse.com

MANOR HOUSE INN

Located just steps from the town's shopping area, Manor House Inn affords the two of you an opportunity to walk to the harbor, explore the town without having to search for a parking place, and then curl up in a cozy, moderately priced guest room.

Situated in a neighborhood of historic homes, Manor House Inn is a three-story gabled, shuttered, and bay-windowed mansion with a fine wraparound porch filled with comfy couches and chairs. The stately structure dates back to 1887 and is listed on the National Register of Historic Places. Sharing the one-acre estate is the former servants' quarters, now called the Chauffeur's Cottage (with three rooms), as well as a collection of other charming cottages.

ROOMS FOR ROMANCE

New since our first visit is Acadia Cottage, whose four rooms boast modern comforts and amenities like large bathrooms with whirlpool tubs. These also have gas fireplaces, queen-sized beds, and wet bars. These rooms are priced in the high $100 to low $200 range.

Another favorite room is Suite A (low $200 range) on the second floor of the refurbished century-old Chauffeur's Cottage. The suite has a large carpeted sitting room with a Victorian couch and chair, a fireplace, and a wet bar. The big, beautiful bedroom, set under skylit eaves, has a king-sized antique bed. The large bathroom has a tub-and-shower combination. A private deck faces the trees.

In the restored main house, our first choice is Room 5 (around $200), known as the Master Bedroom. This front-facing second-floor corner holds a queen-sized bed, a chaise longue, and a fireplace. The large, bright bathroom has a shower and four windows.

Room 7 (mid to high $100 range) is situated under the eaves on the third floor and has a small separate sitting room. There's a shower stall in the bathroom.

Travelers who value complete privacy should be advised that the assigned bathrooms of Rooms 2, 4, and 8 in the main house are across the hall from their respective bedchambers.

THE FACTS

Twelve rooms and four cottage apartment units. Complimentary full breakfast served in dining room at communal table and tables for two. Rates include dinner for two. Free rental bicycles. Disabled access. No minimum stay requirement. Moderate to expensive.

GETTING THERE

From Maine Turnpike (Interstate 95) at Augusta, exit at Route 3 and drive northeast to Belfast, then follow Route 1 north to Route 15 south. Turn right on Route 15 south and follow down Blue Hill peninsula to Deer Isle. Turn right on Main Street (Sunset Road) and follow one block to inn on left.

THE PILGRIM'S INN

Even though it doesn't require a ferry ride, Deer Isle offers visitors a taste of the same quiet, unspoiled atmosphere you'd expect at a more water-bound destination. Much of that atmosphere is provided by the venerable two-century-old Pilgrim's Inn.

Just a short hop by bridge from the mainland, er, Maineland, the inn is a sturdy gambrel-roofed structure with lots of cozy public rooms and the requisite creaky old floors, either polished or painted. The inn, which sports a rooster-red paint job, presides over Mill Pond and adjacent Northwest Harbor, and boasts a fine water-view lawn area with plenty of places to enjoy quiet time together.

Dinners (included in rate) are served at tables for two in the inn's rustic and handsome restaurant paneled with ancient barn wood. Free rental bicycles are also offered to guests.

ROOMS FOR ROMANCE

Not every room fits our definition of romance, since several otherwise enticing accommodations share bathrooms. Rooms 9, 10, 11, 12, and 14 share.

Honeymooners and other guests in-the-know head upstairs to Room 5 (mid $200 range), a large rear corner that overlooks Mill Pond. This room has a cozy full-sized four-poster bed and two wing chairs on pumpkin pine floors. The bathroom has a tub with a hand-held shower attachment.

Another popular accommodation is Room 8 (upper $100 range), a small second-floor corner room with painted pine furniture, a full-sized bed, and a nice view. The bathroom has a tub-and-shower combination.

Room 15 (around $200) is a separate cottage that's a good choice for romantic getaways. The first floor boasts a living room with an open-beam ceiling and a fireplace, a kitchen, a dining area, and a powder room. The bedroom and bathroom are tucked away upstairs.

The Pilgrim's Inn
Main Street (P.O. Box 69)
Deer Isle, ME 04627
Telephone: (207) 348-6615;
toll-free: (888) 778-7505
Web site: www.pilgrimsinn.com

THE FACTS

Nine rooms, each with private bath, deck, and fireplace. Complimentary full breakfast served at tables for two or more. Disabled access. Two-night minimum stay during holiday periods. Closed mid-November through mid-April. Expensive to deluxe.

GETTING THERE

From Interstate 295 north, take exit 31 in Topsham, and follow Route 1 north through Camden. (Route 90 north of Waldboro saves several miles and brings you to Route 1 south of Camden.) Four miles north of Camden Harbor, turn right off Route 1 onto Sunrise Point Road and follow to inn.

THE INN AT SUNRISE POINT
Sunrise Point Road (P.O. Box 1344)
Camden, ME 04843
Telephone: (207) 236-7716
Web site: www.sunrisepoint.com

THE INN AT SUNRISE POINT

As the author of a series of popular bed-and-breakfast inn guides, Jerry Levitin visited thousands of properties from coast to coast before building his own. He knew what worked and what didn't, and when it came to constructing the Inn at Sunrise Point, he made certain everything worked. From the enchanting location to spacious bathrooms with tubs for two and comfy beds positioned to take in the unobstructed Penobscot Bay views, this hideaway rates a perfect ten on our romantic scorecard.

Since our initial visit, ownership has passed to Stephen and Deanna Tallon, natives of Ireland and Australia respectively. The Tallons, veteran international travelers, have nurtured the inn along, introducing new accommodations and places for two to play and relax.

ROOMS FOR ROMANCE

In the main house, there are three moderately sized upstairs rooms, all sporting new private decks offering panoramic Penobscot Bay views. Each room is named after a Maine author. These carry tariffs in the mid $200 to $300 range. Each has a woodburning fireplace, a queen-sized bed, and a bathroom with an extra-long tub big enough for two. The smallest is the middle room, called E. B. White. The May Sarton and Sarah Jewett rooms are nicely windowed corner sites.

The inn's ultimate accommodations are the luxurious cottages (around $500) and a new loft suite (around $400) set against the trees. The cottages offer king-sized beds, oval-shaped spa tubs for two, separate showers, woodburning fireplaces, small refrigerators, coffeemakers, and private decks. In the new bay-windowed loft suite, a king-sized bed sits under a vaulted ceiling and skylight. The two of you will also enjoy the flat-screen TV and DVD player, a large pedestal soaking tub, a steam shower, and a gas stove.

The Fitz Hugh Lane Cottage, situated only ten feet from the water's edge, boasts eye-popping bay views and is prized among honeymooners and other couples in-the-know. The Richard Russo and Edward Hopper cottages are set back a bit farther on the property, but still offer lovely bay views.

The centerpiece of the downstairs public area is a spectacular glass conservatory, in which a full breakfast is served before an equally inviting ocean view.

THE NEWCASTLE INN
River Road
Newcastle, ME 04553
Telephone: (207) 563-5685;
toll-free: (800) 832-8669
Web site: www.newcastleinn.com

THE FACTS

Fifteen rooms, each with private bath. Complimentary full breakfast served in dining room at tables for four. Restaurant. No disabled access. No minimum stay requirement. Expensive to deluxe.

GETTING THERE

Take Maine Turnpike (Interstate 95) to exit 44, which leads to Interstate 295. Take exit 31 from Interstate 295 and turn right onto Route 196 south. Follow for two and a half miles, then take Route 1 and follow through Bath. Seven miles past Wiscasset, turn right on River Road (watch for the Newcastle Inn sign) and follow a half mile to inn on right.

THE NEWCASTLE INN

NEWCASTLE

Our recommendation of the Newcastle Inn sprang initially from the reputation of its dining room as one of the finest—and its hosts as among the most gracious—on the Maine coast. Since our initial travels, Peter and Laura Barclay have not only maintained the inn's reputation as a culinary destination but have done much to create suitably romantic accommodations worthy of an overnight stopover should your travels bring you to Maine's central coast.

The handsome Colonial-style clapboard home stands on a gentle knoll overlooking the Damariscotta Harbor. While many guests choose to unwind close by, the inn's location is convenient for daytripping to popular destinations like Freeport, Boothbay Harbor, Camden, and Pemaquid Point.

Evenings at the inn begin with cocktail hour in a cozy red-walled pub, with complimentary hors d'oeuvres. A wonderful multicourse dinner follows in the inn's French-inspired restaurant, Lupines. Dinners are offered for around $55 per person.

ROOMS FOR ROMANCE

Among the new accommodations created since our first visit is the Portland Head Light Room (around $300). This elegant suite with cathedral ceilings, located in the inn's Cottage Building, has a bedroom with a king-sized bed, a separate living room with a pair of sofas, a large bathroom, a private deck, and a private entry.

Sharing this building is the split-level Cottage (around $200). The lower level holds a living area with a couch. Three steps lead to the bedroom level, presided over by a lovely queen-sized sleigh bed. The bathroom is equipped with a shower.

Another new romantic recommendation is the West Quoddy Room (mid $200 range). A bathroom equipped with a shower and a soaking tub for two separates the bedroom, with its king-sized four-poster bed, and the sitting room, which has chairs, a television, and a gas stove.

The Barclays combined two smaller rooms to create the Matinicus Rock Room (mid $200 range), a spacious retreat with a sitting area furnished with a cushioned love seat and a gas fireplace, and a bathroom featuring a spa-tub-and-shower combination big enough for the two of you.

Also sure to please traveling couples is the Heron Neck Room (mid $200 range), which sits on the third floor and offers great river views. This sunny retreat has a sitting nook with a pair of comfortable chairs and a king-sized four-poster bed.

THE FACTS

Eleven rooms, each with private bath; four rooms with wood-burning fireplaces. Complimentary full breakfast served at tables for two in dining room. Restaurant. No disabled access. Two-night minimum required during holiday periods. Open April through December. Moderate to expensive.

GETTING THERE

From northbound Route 1, seven miles north of bridge at Bath, drive south on Route 144 for eight and a half miles to inn on right.

THE SQUIRE TARBOX INN

One of the most unusual properties we've visited in New England, the Squire Tarbox Inn is a combination working farm and country inn. Consequently, this property should have special appeal to couples who enjoy a casual, relaxing country experience.

A mix of buildings that has evolved eclectically since the mid-1700s, the inn offers guests a range of overnight experiences, from small, countrified rooms to larger, more traditional bed-and-breakfast-style accommodations with fireplaces.

The inn's farm, nurtured by innkeepers Mario and Roni DePietro and their family, boasts two organic vegetable gardens and a brood of chickens that provides fresh eggs for breakfast. The friendly goats are popular with guests. There's also a resident potter.

The inn's two-hundred-year-old lower dining room, with its barn-wood walls and ceiling and a view of Squam Creek, is particularly appealing. At the time of our travels, the inn served multicourse dinners for under $40 per person.

ROOMS FOR ROMANCE

In the property's original Federal-style home, Room 1 (around $200) is a nicely windowed, front-facing corner with a king-sized bed, a love seat, and a working fireplace. The dark wood floor is covered with a braided rug. In the same price range on the second floor is the king-bedded Room 3.

Most honeymooners request rooms in the more rustic barn building. Room 8 (mid $100 range) in the barn sports attractive wallpaper and a low, rough-hewn beam ceiling and supports. Guests here have views of both the front and rear garden areas. The tiny bathroom is equipped with a shower, and the room has entries both from an interior parlor room and from the outside.

We also liked Room 11 (mid $100 range), a cathedral-ceilinged hideaway on the top level of the adjacent carriage-barn building.

We found a few of the smaller accommodations in the barn buildings, with their low ceilings and tiny bathrooms, to be somewhat confining.

THE SQUIRE TARBOX INN
1181 Main Road
Westport Island, ME 04578
Telephone: (207) 882-7693;
toll-free: (800) 818-0626
Web site: www.squiretarboxinn.com

THE FACTS

Sixteen rooms, each with private bath; five with woodburning fireplaces. Complimentary full buffet breakfast served at tables for two. No disabled access. No minimum stay requirement. Closed November through mid-May. Moderate to expensive.

GETTING THERE

From Maine Turnpike (Interstate 95), take exit 52 and follow Interstate 295 north. Take exit 28 and follow Route 1 to Route 27 south. Take Route 96 through East Boothbay. Turn right at yellow light on Murray Hill Road and follow a half mile to inn on right.

FIVE GABLES INN

A century ago, wealthy northeasterners escaped the muggy summers by visiting the more hospitable climes of coastal Maine. Of the numerous seasonal hotels that once catered to those vacationers along the central coast, Five Gables Inn is the sole survivor. Don't expect a sagging relic, however. From the outside to the interior spaces, this crisp, stately hostelry looks as if it could have been built yesterday.

Taking its name from the prominent windowed gables along its front, Five Gables Inn sits on a sloping lawn overlooking Linekin Bay and East Boothbay, a quiet shipbuilding village. Once a twenty-two-room hotel, the structure underwent a tasteful remodeling a few years ago that reduced the number of rooms to sixteen. The furnishings are traditional, and the rooms are carpeted.

ROOMS FOR ROMANCE

Our most highly recommended room and the inn's most popular is Room 14 (low $200 range), where two wing chairs flank a fireplace. There are three windows offering beautiful views of the bay and a king-sized brass-and-iron bed. The skylit bathroom has a shower stall.

Room 11 (mid $100 range) is a nice gabled third-floor corner hideaway that's furnished with a queen-sized bed. We also recommend Rooms 5 and 10 (upper $100 range), two second-floor corners with queen-sized beds and bay views. Room 5 has a brick fireplace. Rooms 6 and 7 also have fireplaces.

Some of the inn's rooms, including Rooms 2, 12, and 15, may prove a bit too small for traveling romantics, and the rooms on the first floor face either the back of the property, lacking a view, or a common front porch, lacking complete privacy if your windows are open.

FIVE GABLES INN
107 Murray Hill Road
East Boothbay, ME 04544
Telephone: (207) 633-4551;
toll-free: (800) 451-5048
Web site: www.fivegablesinn.com

THE FACTS

Six rooms, each with private bath. Complimentary full breakfast served at tables for two. Open all year. Two-night minimum stay during weekends. Moderate to deluxe.

GETTING THERE

From northbound Maine Turnpike (Interstate 95), take exit 25 and follow Route 35/9A south to Kennebunkport. Turn left at the intersection of Routes 9 and 35, cross the bridge, and follow Route 9 east through Kennebunkport. Turn left on Maine Street and follow for approximately one-half mile as Maine curves right and becomes North Street. Turn left on Locke Street and follow to inn.

1802 House
15 Locke Street (P.O. Box 646-A)
Kennebunkport, ME 04046
Telephone: (207) 967-5632;
toll-free: (800) 932-5632
Web site: www.1802inn.com

1802 HOUSE

From the street, 1802 House is unquestionably charming and inviting. However, don't assume that behind the classic New England façade you'll find the creaky floors, dark rooms, and doilies that are typical of so many older homes-turned-inns. 1802 offers sumptuously romantic rooms that would have made the original owners blush.

Set along the peaceful fifteenth fairway of the Cape Arundel golf course, this rambling inn not only serves up large doses of romance but offers regular encounters with the presidents Bush and Florida governor Bush, whose summer estate is just over on the coast and who frequent the links here. It's not uncommon for inn guests to exchange friendly greetings with a passing Bush.

ROOMS FOR ROMANCE

Any inn with a bathroom called the Roman Garden Tub Room gets our immediate attention, and that's what drew us to the luxurious Sebago Room (high $300 range), an obvious favorite of honeymooners and couples celebrating special occasions. When guests here aren't enjoying the tub room, with its corner raised spa tub for two set in an Italian tile surround, and the deck accessed through French doors, they can enjoy a separate sitting room with a sofa and a gas fireplace, and a bedroom with a queen-sized four-poster bed draped with gauzy organza. A separate bathroom holds a shower built for two.

We also recommend Arundel (high $200 range), a lovely room with wallpaper, a beamed ceiling, a woodburning fireplace, and a queen-sized four-poster bed. The bathroom has a spa tub for two and a separate shower.

Another romantic choice is Windsor (high $200 range), furnished with a striking queen-sized curved canopied bed, wing chairs, a brick fireplace, and a bathroom with a spa tub big enough for two.

The reasonably priced York Room (high $100 range) has a spa tub for two, great morning-sun exposure, and a queen-sized bed.

THE FACTS

Sixteen rooms, each with private bath. Complimentary full breakfast served at communal tables. Complimentary afternoon refreshments. Open all year. No disabled access. Two-night minimum stay required during weekends. Moderate to deluxe.

GETTING THERE

From northbound Maine Turnpike (Interstate 95), take exit 25 and follow Route 35/9A south to Kennebunkport. Turn left at intersection of Routes 9 and 35 and follow Route 35 south for one and seven-tenths miles to traffic light at intersection of Route 1. Cross over Route 1 and bear right, continuing on Route 35 south/9A. Follow into lower Kennebunk village to traffic light at intersection of Route 9 east. Turn left and follow over drawbridge to monument. Turn right on Ocean Avenue and left on Green Street. Follow to inn on left.

CAPTAIN LORD MANSION
6 Pleasant Street (P.O. Box 800)
Kennebunkport, ME 04046
Telephone: (207) 967-3141;
toll-free: (800) 522-3141
Web site: www.captainlord.com

CAPTAIN LORD MANSION

While many of the inns featured in *Weekends for Two in New England* have been around for well over a century, those who operate them aren't known for their longevity. In fact, the majority of properties we've featured have passed to new owners in the few short years since our first edition was published.

Notable exceptions are Bev Davis and Rick Litchfield, who have been at the helm of the Captain Lord Mansion for over twenty-five years. It was back in 1978 when Rick and Bev, former McDonald's Corporation staffers, ventured into Kennebunkport and were overcome by the sight of this stately historic cupola-capped mansion that had been functioning as a home for elderly mid-coast Maine women. After the ink on the contract had dried, Rick recalls being left with a bank account holding all of $15.

The inn enjoys a quintessential Maine setting on a long, maple-shaded lawn in a delightful mature neighborhood adjacent to a village green and overlooking the Kennebunk River. Inside are charming vestiges of yesteryear, including a dining room table and chairs belonging to the mansion's namesake family, the Lords. The original 1812 cooking fireplace is another historic centerpiece.

ROOMS FOR ROMANCE

For all intents and purposes, history stops at the doors of the guest rooms, which boast tasteful contemporary touches like lighted makeup mirrors, wall soundproofing, double vanities, tubs for two, and bathrooms with heated floors.

A favorite romantic hideaway is the Champion Suite (high $300 range), a second-floor corner room with a hand-painted European-style king-sized bed and a very comfortable sitting area with a couch and chair. The bathroom is a destination in and of itself, boasting a Roman column–flanked tub for two and a separate marble shower built for two.

Another stunning bathroom with a spa tub for two is found behind the doors of the fabulous Oriental Suite (high $300 range), which also boasts a massive king-sized canopy bed and a gas fireplace.

The Ship Merchant Suite (around $500) ranks as one of the most romantic rooms in New England. One of those spaces that must be seen to be truly appreciated, the suite consists of three rooms, including two ultra-romantic bath areas. One has a shower with a waterfall, and the other holds exercise equipment and a lavish spa tub for two set in front of a gas fireplace.

The Excelsior Suite (around $400) is a handsome corner hideaway with a king-sized four-poster bed, at the foot of which is a cozy seating area with a couch and a cushy chair set before a fireplace. The bathroom has a heated marble floor and a spa-tub-and-shower combination.

The Americana Suite (high $200 range) is a spacious, nicely wallpapered third-floor accommodation with a king-sized bed and a sitting area.

THE FACTS

Four rooms, each with private bath. Complimentary full breakfast served at a communal table. Complimentary afternoon refreshments. No disabled access. Two-night minimum stay required. Closed November through April. Expensive to deluxe.

GETTING THERE

From Maine Turnpike (Interstate 95), take exit 25 and follow Route 35/9A south to Kennebunkport. Turn left at the intersection of Routes 9 and 35, cross the bridge, and follow Route 9 east through Dock Square. Continue on Route 9 to Goose Rock Beach. At Bradbury's Market, leave Route 9 and continue straight onto Pier Road. Follow for two-tenths of a mile to inn on right.

THE INN AT HARBOR HEAD

After touring the best of Kennebunkport's impressive collection of romantic inns and small hotels, we decided to bypass the more obvious choices and feature a couple of gems off the beaten track.

It took us two visits to Kennebunkport to discover the Inn at Harbor Head, which boasts an idyllic setting beside the glassy waters of Cape Porpoise Harbor. Although only a three-minute car ride from the inn, the bustling village of Kennebunkport might as well be a hundred miles away. Under new ownership since our first visit, the inn is on a quiet residential street, and the postcard view of the harbor and the lobster boats is a treat.

ROOMS FOR ROMANCE

You'll be treated to a fine harbor view through the French doors of the Garden Room (mid $200 range), a small, first-floor accommodation that features a Japanese theme. One of our favorite rooms, Garden holds a queen-sized four-poster bed with a harbor view, and a tiny bathroom with a shower stall. There's also a private water-view deck.

Although you won't see the water from the green-paneled Greenery Room (upper $200 range), you can soak in the warm water of the rose-colored spa tub for two in the beautiful mirrored and green-tiled bathroom.

In the second-floor Ocean Room (around $200), a handsome queen-sized pineapple-post plantation bed is placed diagonally near a cozy love seat. This room offers a water view during the winter months, when the leaves are off the trees.

Our favorite room is the Summer Suite (low $300 range), accessed by a private stairway from the library. Five windows boast a grand water vista, and the spacious room is furnished with a wicker chaise and love seat and a king-sized bed with a matching wicker headboard. The room also contains the inn's most sumptuous bathroom, a cathedral-ceilinged retreat that holds a step-up ocean-view spa tub for two, a marble vanity, and a bidet.

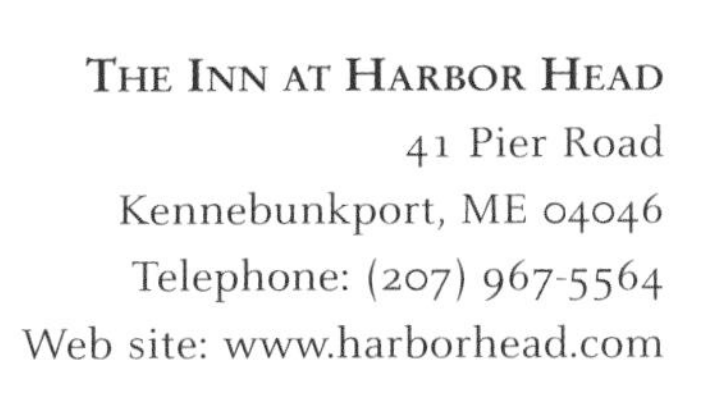

THE INN AT HARBOR HEAD
41 Pier Road
Kennebunkport, ME 04046
Telephone: (207) 967-5564
Web site: www.harborhead.com

THE FACTS

Six rooms, each with private bath; two with gas fireplaces. Complimentary full breakfast served at a communal table or in your room. Complimentary afternoon refreshments. Wireless Internet service. No disabled access. Two-night minimum stay required during weekends and holiday periods. Moderate to deluxe.

GETTING THERE

From southbound Maine Turnpike (Interstate 95), take exit 19 and turn left on Route 9 east. Turn left at light and follow Route 9 east as it forks right. At second traffic light, turn left on Route 35 north. Inn entry (Bufflehead Cove Road) is approximately one-half mile on right.

BUFFLEHEAD COVE INN

As we made our way along the unmarked gravel drive from Highway 35 and caught our first glimpse of Bufflehead Cove Inn, it was as if we had discovered a pirate's map to hidden treasure. After snuggling into one of New England's most romantic rooms, we considered keeping this sensual secret to ourselves.

It's not without selfish reluctance that we share with readers this memory-making discovery, which ranks as a definitive example of a romantic getaway.

An attractive three-story gray-shingled home with white trim, the inn overlooks the serene Kennebunk River, whose gentle waters rise and fall with the Atlantic tides. Members of the Bush family, whose summer compound is nearby, are among the local fishermen who troll the shallow waters here.

The inn is operated by longtime gracious innkeepers Jim and Harriet Gott, southern Maine natives who generously share their travel tips with guests.

ROOMS FOR ROMANCE

A glassed-in balcony with a table for two and a chaise is the highlight of the impressive Balcony Room (low $300 range), enlarged since our last visit and furnished with a king-sized bed, a spa tub for two, and a private bath with a custom-tiled shower. Paintings by a Maine artist adorn the walls.

Next door, the River Room (high $100 range) holds a queen-sized bed from which the two of you can view the water. A private little balcony has a water view.

The room in which we stayed, Hideaway (mid $300 range), is a heavenly cottagelike suite connected to the inn by one wall. Carpeted in wool and exquisitely decorated with art, a bookshelf, and plants, the spacious suite consists of a sleeping area with a king-sized bed and a sitting area with a couch. The two environments are separated by a custom-tiled two-sided gas fireplace. Windows on three sides of the suite offer views of the adjacent woods, garden, and river. Guests here are also treated to a private porch.

Hideaway's luxurious bathroom, the size of an average guest room, boasts a deep corner-mounted spa tub for two under a skylight, a separate glass shower stall, and beautiful custom tile. A brass candelabra at the edge of the tub adds a crowning romantic touch.

The River Cottage (high $300 range), located in an attractive separate building, is a spacious romantic hideaway with a kitchen, a living room with a towering Palladian window, a fireplace, two couches, and a spa tub for two, as well as a glassed-in shower. You'll climb winding stairs to reach the tantalizing loft bedroom furnished with a king-sized bed and an expansive water-view window.

BUFFLEHEAD COVE INN
Route 35 (P.O. Box 499)
Kennebunkport, ME 04046
Telephone: (207) 967-3879
Web site: www.buffleheadcove.com

DAYTIME DIVERSIONS

While visiting MANCHESTER, the two of you might consider a trip to the Southern Vermont Arts Center's four hundred acres on the slope of Mount Equinox. Here you'll find hiking trails, a botany trail, and sculpture gardens.

The New England Maple Museum and Maple Market, the largest establishment of its kind in the world, is located on Route 7 in RUTLAND, near our destinations in Chittenden and Woodstock. Rutland is also home to a Norman Rockwell museum.

Locally made gourmet goodies, clothing, and products are sold at the Stowe Foliage Crafts Fair, usually held the last week of September in STOWE.

CHITTENDEN, WOODSTOCK, and LUDLOW are within easy reach of the Killington, Bromley, and Pico ski areas.

Vermont's oldest professional theater is located in WESTON, between Grafton and Ludlow.

Last but not least, Ben and Jerry's Ice Cream Factory, open for tours and tasting, is located on Route 100, just north of Waitsfield in WATERBURY.

TABLES FOR TWO

The Governor's Inn and the Old Tavern, both of which are described in this section, have their own highly rated dining rooms.

T.J. BUCKLEY'S, Brattleboro (near West Chesterfield, NH)
BISTRO HENRY, Manchester
INN AT WESTVIEW FARM, Dorset
THE DANIELS HOUSE CAFÉ (lunch), Grafton
RASPBERRIES AND THYME, Chester

VERMONT

THE FACTS

Nine rooms, each with private bathroom, double-sided fireplace, shower, and spa tub for two. Complimentary full breakfast served at tables for two. Complimentary evening refreshments. Two-night minimum stay required during weekends and foliage season; three-night stay required during holiday weekends; four-night minimum stay during winter high season. Disabled access. Closed early April to early May and mid-November to early December. Deluxe.

GETTING THERE

From Interstate 89, take exit 10 toward Waterbury and Stowe. Then follow Route 100 north for eleven miles. In village of Stowe, turn left at traffic light on Route 108 (Mountain Road). Follow for three miles and turn right on Houston Farm Road. Turn left at first driveway to inn.

STONE HILL INN

The "new school" of innkeeping is how Hap and Amy Jordan proudly describe their approach to hospitality at this wonderful treasure in the Vermont woods. "We wanted to create the type of experience for our guests that we seek when we travel," recalls Amy, a hotel concierge during a previous life. "We love the small size, intimacy, and interaction with the innkeepers you find at country inns and bed-and-breakfast inns, but we don't always enjoy the lack of amenities and sometimes lack of privacy between rooms."

For the Jordans, embracing the "new school" meant creating a brand new inn—one that combines the best features of luxury hotels with the small size, personal attention, and unique décor that a B&B provides. At Stone Hill Inn, this translates to such thoughtful touches as fireside spa tubs for two in each of the nine guest rooms, double sinks, separate showers, king-sized beds, places for the two of you to sit, and soundproofing between rooms.

The setting was also important, and Stone Hill Inn enjoys a secluded scenic hilltop spot midway between popular Stowe Mountain Resort and the picture-perfect village of Stowe.

ROOMS FOR ROMANCE

Save for tastefully unique decorating touches and views, the rooms at Stone Hill Inn feature similar amenities that romantic travelers will certainly find appealing. Dual-sided fireplaces can be seen from both the king-sized beds and from the spa tubs for two that grace each bathroom. Rooms are similarly sized and also feature upscale furnishings, double vanity sinks, separate showers, and big sliding doors opening to the inn's grounds.

Arguably the most romantic room is Catamount, with its enticing canopied bed and contrasting dark window drapes. The Sterling and Cotton Brook rooms boast views of the water garden and waterfall, while the White Birch Room is done up in tasteful shades of cranberry, teal, and taupe.

Rates run from the mid $200 range in the spring to the mid and high $300 range during high season (fall and winter).

STONE HILL INN
89 Houston Farm Road
Stowe, VT 05672
Telephone: (802) 253-6282
Web site: www.stonehillinn.com

Rabbit Hill Inn
48 Lower Waterford Road
(P.O. Box 55)
Lower Waterford, VT 05848
Telephone: (802) 748-5168;
toll-free: (800) 762-8669
Web site: www.rabbithillinn.com

THE FACTS

Nineteen rooms, each with private bath. Complimentary full breakfast served at tables for two. Swimming pond. Pub. Dining room serving multicourse fixed-price dinners with advance reservations. Disabled access. Two-night minimum stay required during weekends for some rooms; two- to three-night minimum during holiday periods. Closed early April, early November, and Christmas. Expensive to deluxe.

GETTING THERE

Lower Waterford is located near junction of Interstates 91 and 93. From Interstate 91, take exit 19 to Interstate 93 south. Take exit 1 and turn right onto Route 18 south. Drive seven miles to inn on right. From northbound Interstate 93, take exit 44 and turn left onto Route 18 north. Drive two miles to inn on left.

RABBIT HILL INN

Set near the New Hampshire border less than an hour's drive from Canada, Rabbit Hill is our northernmost Vermont destination. But the distance from New England's major metropolitan areas only adds to the inn's allure.

We arrived road-weary on a chilly afternoon, but tea and pastries, glowing fires, and soft music quickly set a warm, inviting mood. Fixed-price dinners (just shy of $50 per person at the time of our travels) bring most guests back together again in the evening.

The inn spans two Federal-period buildings. The columned three-story main house dates from the 1820s; the smaller wing was added about thirty years later as a ballroom. Each has been refurbished with loving care.

ROOMS FOR ROMANCE

Your hearts will flutter on entering the Loft (low $300 range), accessed via its own stairway. This spacious room is set under an eave and holds a king-sized canopied bed. A comfy couch faces a gas fireplace, and nearby an artful Palladian-crowned window grouping overlooks the backyard and a wooded area beyond. The polished pine floors are covered with hand-hooked rugs. There's also a private outdoor deck and a second sitting area with two Boston rockers. Through a tiny step-up dressing area, you'll enter a large bathroom that holds a big white spa tub for two and a separate shower stall.

High on the third floor is our favorite: the grand Jonathan Cummings suite (mid $300 range). Guests entering this spacious suite will find a queen-sized canopy bed facing a gas-log fireplace. Turn the corner and you'll enter a large dressing room with a sitting and reading area and a relaxing and romantic spa tub for two placed in front of a second fireplace. There's also a screened and furnished porch with White Mountain views.

For a night in rustic elegance, the two of you might sample the popular Cedar Glen (low $300 range), an unusual accommodation reminiscent of a Vermont country cabin trimmed with cedar and pine. There's a fireplace, a nice mountain view from expansive windows, a large sitting area, and a spa tub for two. You'll retire to a king-sized canopy bed crafted from peeled logs.

THE FACTS

Twelve rooms, each with private bath. Complimentary full breakfast served in dining room at tables for four, six, and eight. Complimentary afternoon refreshments. Swimming pool. Game room. No disabled access. Smoking is not permitted. Two-night minimum during holiday periods. Moderate to deluxe.

GETTING THERE

From northbound Interstate 89, take exit 9 and follow south to Middlesex and onto Route 100 B. Follow to Route 100 and drive south to Waitsfield. Turn left on Bridge Street, pass over a covered bridge, and bear right at fork onto East Warren Road. Follow one mile to inn on left.

THE INN AT THE ROUND BARN FARM
1661 East Warren Road
Waitsfield, VT 05673
Telephone: (802) 496-2276
Web site: www.theroundbarn.com

THE INN AT THE ROUND BARN FARM

New England travelers who make a day trip to that famous Waterbury, Vermont, ice cream factory and then drive straight home are savoring only part of the treat. After a tour and taste, in-the-know couples head south just a few miles to a sumptuous hideaway that is to romantic inns what Ben and Jerry's is to gourmet ice cream.

The distinctive twelve-sided Shaker barn—one of just a few left in Vermont—is the establishment's signature structure, but it's what's inside the adjacent buildings that lures lovers to the Inn at the Round Barn Farm.

ROOMS FOR ROMANCE

The Joslin Room (high $200 range), for example, sports walls painted a deep seductive cranberry. The king-sized bed is covered with a canopy, and the large bathroom is outfitted with a tub for two and a steam shower.

Since our first visit, the innkeepers have renovated the second-floor Jones Room (around $200), a large and cozy space set under a sloping ceiling with exposed rustic beams. There's a romantic mountain-and-garden view from the queen-sized brass bed through a floor-mounted window. The bathroom holds a shower stall.

Guests will likely be quite satisfied with the aforementioned guest rooms, but we must admit to being smitten with four unbelievable romantic chambers that occupy what was originally the hayloft of an attached barn structure. The Sherman, Dana, English, and Richardson rooms (mid $200 range) will take your breath away. But reserve well in advance; these rooms are coveted.

In our opinion, the most romantic room in the house is the newly renovated Richardson Room (high $200 range), a fresh and spacious hideaway with a row of floor-mounted mountain-view windows and a skylight. In addition to a lovely gas fireplace and a partially canopied king-sized bed, there's a cushy chaise and a love seat for cuddling. The bright step-down bath area holds a long spa tub for two set in a wooden frame and placed under windows with a pretty view. There's also a glass-enclosed shower stall.

Next door is the cathedral-ceilinged English Room. This impressive room has a king-sized bed and a sitting area furnished with a love seat set before a gas fireplace. The windows afford soothing views of the surrounding hills, and the bathroom has a large steam shower for two.

The equally tasteful Sherman and Dana rooms also boast gas fireplaces, romantic vistas, and steam showers for two.

The Abbott Room (low $300 range), new since our first visit, is a spacious suite with a private sitting room complete with a hot tub and a fireplace. The Terrace Room sits below ground next to a game room that's equipped with a pool table, an organ, and couches and chairs.

A sixty-foot-long lap swimming pool runs through the historic round barn and into an adjacent greenhouse.

Fox Creek Inn
Chittenden Dam Road
Chittenden, VT 05737
Telephone: (802) 483-6213
Web site: www.foxcreekinn.com

THE FACTS

Nine rooms, each with private bath. Rates include full dinner and breakfast served in a communal dining room. Complimentary refreshments served every evening. Smoking is not permitted. Two-night minimum stay required during weekends; two- to three-night minimum required during holiday periods. Expensive to deluxe.

GETTING THERE

From northbound Route 7 just north of Rutland, pass red brick power station (on your left) and follow East Pittsburgh Road, which eventually becomes Chittenden Dam Road. Follow road for approximately six miles. Just past the fire station, drive straight for a half mile to inn on the left. For more detailed driving instructions from New York or Boston, request a map when making your reservation.

FOX CREEK INN

Some traveling romantics we know seek out only those getaway destinations that allow them to disappear immediately into the woodwork and savor each other's exclusive company. For these folks, the "do not disturb" sign is always out, and breakfast arrives at their door on a tray.

For other couples, the romance of the road includes a chance to mingle with innkeepers and share a meal or conversation with fellow sojourners before retiring to a private guest room.

Those who find the latter experience appealing will savor every moment of a visit to Fox Creek Inn, a delightful retreat hidden away in the Green Mountains of central Vermont.

Painted a soothing green and sporting white shutters and an inviting front porch, the structure was built more than 150 years ago as a farmhouse, and later was acquired by a colleague of Thomas Edison. Edison and Henry Ford are among the luminaries who have spent a night or two here. Since our first visit, the inn passed to new owners who changed the name from Tulip Tree Inn to Fox Creek Inn.

The inn is located off the beaten path several miles from the closest town, but guests needn't worry about hopping in the car to search for a suitable restaurant. Both dinner and breakfast are included in the Fox Creek's rates, which start in the mid to upper $200 range per couple.

ROOMS FOR ROMANCE

The inn's most romantic lodging is Room 9 (around $300), a large accommodation with a spa tub for two, a shower for two, and fireplaces in both the bathroom and bedroom.

Another favorite is Room 4 (mid $200 range), windowed on three sides and offering views of the trees. The room has pine flooring and is equipped with a king-sized bed, two chairs, and a spa tub set in a polished wood frame in the middle of the bathroom. The wallpapered bathroom also contains double sinks.

Room 3, a front-facing corner, holds a queen-sized bed and two wing chairs. The bathroom here is fitted with a spa tub for two.

Located less than twenty miles from Killington, the inn is a popular destination among Vermont ski enthusiasts. During warmer months, the romantic sound of an adjacent brook wafts through open windows of the inn's front-facing rooms.

THE FACTS

Eleven rooms and four suites, each with private bath. Complimentary full breakfast served at communal table. Complimentary evening libations and hors d'oeuvres. Restaurant. Swimming pond. Disabled access. Two-night minimum stay required during weekends and holiday periods. Moderate to deluxe.

GETTING THERE

From Boston (153 miles), follow Interstate 93 north to Interstate 89, then north to Vermont. Take exit 1 and follow Route 4 west through Woodstock and another mile and a half to inn on right.

THE JACKSON HOUSE INN

From the road, the historic farmhouse may look like just another example of a grandmotherly, quaint bed-and-breakfast inn. But most grandmas could only dream of living like this; the Jackson House Inn is one of the most exquisite inns we've discovered anywhere in New England.

This luxurious property represents more than a decade of careful and deliberate nurturing by friendly innkeepers Carl and Linda Delnegro. The two have created fifteen delightfully distinctive rooms and suites, whose captivating environs complement this particularly enchanting part of Vermont. Your room for the night might hold bronze statuary, silk wall coverings, French crystal, or Chinese porcelain. Many guest chambers have views of the inn's rambling five-acre garden.

ROOMS FOR ROMANCE

The inn's most indulgent accommodations are the spacious one-room suites (mid to upper $300 range), which offer king-sized beds, fireplaces, CD players, French doors, and sky-lit bathrooms with massage tubs for two.

A favorite among traveling romantics, Cranberry (mid $200 range) features mauve-colored silk wall coverings, Oriental rugs, a queen-sized, four-poster bed, and a veranda accessed via French doors.

Francesca and Nicholas is a decadent hideaway that reportedly cost some thirty thousand dollars to decorate. Furnishings include a queen-sized cherry sleigh bed handsomely detailed with wicker, an upholstered sofa, and a wing chair. The private balcony overlooks the expansive backyard.

The award-winning gardens provide many quiet spots for two, and the backyard has a swimming pond with a gleaming beach of crushed marble. The inn also offers an intimate garden-view restaurant that has earned outstanding reviews.

The Jackson House Inn has a Woodstock address, but the fabled village, a mile or so to the east, is not within walking distance.

THE JACKSON HOUSE INN
114-3 Senior Lane
Woodstock, VT 05091
Telephone: (802) 457-2065
Web site: www.jacksonhouse.com

Andrie Rose Inn
13 Pleasant Street
Ludlow, VT 05149
Telephone: (802) 228-4846;
toll-free: (800) 223-4846
Web site: www.andrieroseinn.com

THE FACTS

Twenty rooms, each with private bath, most with tubs for two. Complimentary full breakfast (not included with all rooms) served in dining room at tables for two or delivered to certain rooms. Complimentary evening refreshments. Four-course dinner served Fridays and Saturdays by reservation. Bar. Complimentary bicycle rentals. No disabled access. Two-night minimum stay required during winter weekends and holiday periods. Moderate to deluxe.

GETTING THERE

From northbound Interstate 91, exit at Route 103 (exit 6) in Rockingham and follow Route 103 north to Ludlow, where Route 103 becomes Main Street. Turn left on Depot Street and drive one block to inn on corner of Depot and Pleasant Streets.

ANDRIE ROSE INN

Vermont skiers who remember Ms. Andrie Rose's Pleasant Street Guest Lodge wouldn't recognize the place these days. What was once a small, homespun winter refuge in the shadow of Okemo Mountain has evolved into an enchanting estate with guest rooms that rank among Vermont's most romantic.

ROOMS FOR ROMANCE

An 1820s-era farmhouse is at the heart of the compound. The shingled and shuttered home, completely restored, contains nine guest rooms as well as the inn's public rooms.

Our two favorites in the main house are Skylight and Mountain View (around $200), set at the rear of the inn under the eaves on the second floor. Both have spa tubs for two. In Skylight, a queen-sized bed sits on rose-colored carpeting under an angled skylight. Mountain View, which also features a skylight, is equipped with a queen-sized antique carved bed from which you'll be able to gaze at Okemo Mountain.

Three other romantic main-house rooms are Country Lace, Country Roses, and Sunrise, each of which is equipped with a tiled and wainscoted oval spa tub for two. Sunrise is a small room equipped with a queen-sized bed. These hideaways carry rates in the $200 range.

Romantics who value privacy might find the first-floor Village Way Room situated a bit too close to the public areas.

The Solitude Building holds seven luxury suites (mid $300 range), each individually decorated with designer linens and wallcoverings. Onyx spa tubs for two are placed in the bedrooms, along with plush robes. Some have steam showers. These rooms have king-sized beds, custom furnishings, antiques, videocassette players, CD players, and refrigerators.

A higher level of luxury and romance is offered in the separate guest house behind the main house, in which four mouthwatering suites await. Each has a gas fireplace, a spa tub for two, a television, and a videocassette player.

Two single-bedroom suites (around $300) occupy the top floor. Outrage, the first, holds a couple of overstuffed and oversized chairs with ottomans whose upholstery matches the bed and window coverings. A gas fireplace flickers within sight of a king-sized canopied iron bed. The exquisitely wallpapered and marbled bathroom holds a large whirlpool tub under a window and a separate marble shower.

Next door is Double Diamond, which features a blue and white color scheme, white wicker furnishings, and a canopied queen-sized bed, also of wicker. It has similar luxury appointments.

The ground floor consists of a pair of elegant two-bedroom, one-and-a-half-bath suites with kitchens (around $500), which might work for two couples traveling together.

THE FACTS

Nine rooms, each with private bath. Complimentary full breakfast. Complimentary afternoon refreshments. Dinner served most Saturdays and certain other evenings by reservation. Full bar. Vermont country picnic lunches available at extra cost. No disabled access. Two-night minimum stay required on weekends during peak season. Moderate to deluxe.

GETTING THERE

From northbound Interstate 91, exit at Route 103 (exit 6) in Rockingham and follow Route 103 north to Ludlow, where Route 103 becomes Main Street. Inn is on left.

The Governor's Inn
86 Main Street
Ludlow, VT 05149
Telephone: (802) 228-8830;
toll-free: (800) 468-3766
Web site: www.thegovernorsinn.com

THE GOVERNOR'S INN

Vermont-bound travelers for whom a memorable romantic getaway must combine fine food and lodging under one roof will be hard-pressed to top the Governor's Inn. At this venerable destination, meals are part of the romantic experience.

The inn is a historic three-story home on Main Street at the edge of Ludlow's downtown district. It was built in 1890 by William Stickney as a gift for his wife, Lizzie. Eight years later, Stickney became governor of Vermont.

Since our first visit, the inn was acquired by Jim and Cathy Kubec, who left careers in engineering and nursing, respectively, and have made wholesale improvements to the property.

ROOMS FOR ROMANCE

Most of the inn's guest rooms and bathrooms are comparatively small, but each room is decorated handsomely with European antiques and pretty wall coverings. One of our favorites is Priscilla's Room (mid $200 range), a more spacious corner hideaway carpeted in deep green and furnished with an attractive corner gas fireplace and a queen-sized antique burled screen. The small bathroom contains a tub-and-shower combination.

In the cozy suite (low $300 range) set under the eaves, a queen-sized four-poster bed sits at the center of the room adjacent to a sloping skylight with views of Okemo Mountain. There's also a sitting room and a spa tub for two set beneath a skylight.

The side-facing Governor's Room (mid $200 range) features a bay window set with two antique chairs. There's also a gas fireplace and a tiny bathroom with a shower stall.

Facing front on the third floor is Jessica's Room (mid $200 range), a wallpapered, rose-carpeted room with a king-sized bed under a skylight. A telescope offers a view of Okemo Mountain. This room, a favorite honeymoon hideaway, also boasts a gas stove and a remodeled bathroom with a spa tub for two.

For romantic getaways, we do not recommend Laura's Room, whose bathroom is across the hall.

The Governor's Inn continues to earn wide recognition as one of Vermont's finest restaurants. Cathy is a graduate of Connecticut Culinary Institute, and her guests take their meals in a redecorated dining room at private tables set with silver, crystal, and antique china. At the time of our travels, fixed-price dinners were offered on certain evenings for about $50 per person.

THE FACTS

Five rooms, each with private bath. Complimentary full breakfast served at communal tables. Complimentary afternoon refreshments. No disabled access. Two-night minimum stay during weekends; two- to three-night minimum during holiday periods. Expensive to deluxe.

GETTING THERE

From Route 7 in Manchester Center, drive north on Route 30 for six miles to inn on right, just south of Dorset village green.

Cornucopia of Dorset
3228 Route 30
Dorset, VT 05251
Telephone: (802) 867-5751;
toll-free: (800) 566-5751
Web site: www.cornucopiaofdorset.com

CORNUCOPIA OF DORSET

As much as we look forward to a visit to lovely Manchester, the stores, cars, and shopping hordes eventually produce a yearning for those sleepy, romantic villages Vermont is so well known for. Dorset, just six miles north of the outlet centers, is a quick drive from Manchester, yet far enough away to possess a distinctly quieter atmosphere. It's also the site of Cornucopia of Dorset, a charming home base for southern Vermont wanderings.

Located along Route 30 within earshot of the village church chimes, the Colonial-style inn is fairly small, offering only five rooms, including a cozy cottage. There are also many comfortable public spaces in the main house, providing couples with opportunities for added relaxation. Breakfast is served at communal tables in a spacious dining room.

ROOMS FOR ROMANCE

One of Vermont's coziest lovers' hideaways is the Owl's Head cottage. Offered for around $300 per night, this former carriage house is a freestanding shuttered jewel set at the rear of the property against tall trees. On ground level, a love seat and a chair sit on pine floors before a woodburning brick fireplace. Adjacent to the comfy seating area is a full kitchen. The bathroom has a tub-and-shower combination. French doors open to a private patio facing an expansive back lawn. Upstairs is a carpeted loft containing skylights and a queen-sized bed.

The main house contains four guest rooms. The Scallop (around $200) is a second-floor corner room with a woodburning brick fireplace, a queen-sized canopied bed, tall windows, and a spacious and sunny bathroom holding a tub-and-shower combination.

Our other favorite, Green Peak (around $200), occupies a second-floor corner and is equipped with a queen-sized pencil-post bed and a large bathroom. A picture window affords pretty views of the backyard with its lawn, sugar maple trees, and gardens.

Dorset Hill (around $200) has a king-sized bed that can convert to two twins, and a small step-up bath with a shower stall. Mother Myrick (around $200) is a smaller, king-bedded room with built-in bookcases and a bathroom containing double sinks.

THE FACTS

Thirty-two rooms, each with private bath. Complimentary full breakfast. Dinner available in inn's restaurant. Bar. Gift shop. No disabled access. Moderate to deluxe.

GETTING THERE

From northbound Interstate 91, exit at Route 30 in Brattleboro, VT, and follow north to intersection with Route 11. Turn left and follow Route 11/30 west for one and a half miles past Route 7 to Manchester. Turn left at blinking light on Route 7A and follow to inn on right.

THE VILLAGE COUNTRY INN
Historic Route 7A
Manchester Village, VT 05254
Telephone: (802) 362-1792;
toll-free: (800) 370-0300
Web site: www.villagecountryinn.com

THE VILLAGE COUNTRY INN

Whether its long roofline is glistening under a fresh dusting of snow, its fine porch is sprinkled with crisp new-fallen leaves, or its rear gardens are shimmering in summer sunlight, the Village Country Inn possesses all the ingredients for casting one of New England's most romantic spells.

One of the gracious vintage edifices that contribute to Manchester Village's famous charm, the inn has been a part of the community for generations. And though it's a village landmark, the Village Country Inn doesn't simply offer enchanting curb appeal. Innkeepers Lizanne and Jay Degen, who have owned the inn since the mid-1980s, have created romantic interior spaces that weren't available to visitors in the old days.

Over the past decade or so, the couple has removed walls to enlarge rooms, infused guest chambers with pretty wall and window coverings, and improved outdoor living spaces.

ROOMS FOR ROMANCE

The rooms here are classified as either standard or as "larger special accommodations." We recommend the latter group, whose rates, which include breakfast, vary from the mid $100 range to around $300 per night.

In the "larger special" category, there are three types of rooms to choose from: garden rooms, large luxury rooms, and suites. Garden rooms on the ground floor have private outdoor entrances, king- or queen-sized canopy beds, and televisions and telephones.

The large luxury rooms, on the second and third floors, have king-sized or queen-sized beds, many of which have canopies. Several of these rooms have fireplaces. The front-facing Room 106, for example, has a rose color scheme and contains a queen-sized iron bed with a lace canopy. A love seat sits at the foot of the bed. The spacious carpeted bathroom has a rounded glass shower and a small, old-fashioned tub on a tiled pedestal.

Among the inn's suites is Room 221 on the third floor, overlooking the gardens, the gazebo, and the swimming pool. Situated within earshot of a gentle fountain, the large bedroom is illuminated by four windows. The king-sized bed and the chaise longue have matching fabric. A bathroom with a pedestal tub and a round shower separates the bedroom from a corner sitting room with wicker furnishings.

Since the inn faces the village's main thoroughfare, we recommend the side- or rear-facing rooms to guests bothered by traffic noise.

1811 House
Route 7A (P.O. Box 39)
Manchester Village, VT 05254
Telephone: (802) 362-1811;
toll-free: (800) 432-1811
Web site: www.1811house.com

THE FACTS

Thirteen rooms, each with private bath. Complimentary full breakfast served at communal tables and tables for two. Wireless Internet service. No disabled access. Two-night minimum stay required during weekends and foliage season; three-night minimum during some holiday, special-event, or foliage weekends. Moderate to expensive.

GETTING THERE

From northbound Interstate 91, take exit 2 (Route 30 north). This joins with Route 11 and leads into Manchester. At "T" junction at Route 7A, turn left and follow Route 7A for just over one mile to inn on left.

1811 HOUSE

Set on seven-plus lush acres in the shadow of a spired church, 1811 House is our top choice for a Manchester Village romantic rendezvous.

Its name suggests a nineteenth-century vintage, but the structure, one of the community's oldest, was actually built in the 1770s. It was converted from a home to an inn in 1811 and has welcomed guests ever since, except for a time when it served as the home of Mary Lincoln Isham, granddaughter of Abraham Lincoln.

The inn boasts multiple antique-furnished public rooms, two of which have fireplaces, and there's a basement recreation room with Ping-Pong and billiard tables. A small English-style pub (called a "snug") with a shiny wood bar is warmed by yet another fireplace. Oriental rugs are placed throughout the inn.

ROOMS FOR ROMANCE

In addition to the handsome Federal-style home, the property has a separate cottage containing three rooms. One of these, the cozy second-floor Mary Olson Room (mid $200 range), is set under a wallpapered sloping ceiling and features a fireplace and two leather chairs. Most of the inn's rooms lack couches or love seats but have matching chairs.

Also in the cottage is the Lang Room (mid $200 range), a romantic lamp-lit corner site with several tall windows, a brick- and wood-paneled fireplace, and a king-sized bed with a fishnet canopy.

In the main house, the handsome Robinson Room (mid $200 range) on the second floor is the fall favorite because of its beautiful view. From your private porch, you can see across the length of the back lawn and gardens, over a pond and golf course to the distant Green Mountains. The room has a king-sized canopied bed and a bathroom with a clawfoot tub enclosed in marble.

In the Mary Lincoln Isham Room (mid $200 range), two tall windows flank a wood-and-marble fireplace. A queen-sized canopied bed sits nearby.

Trimmed tastefully in red, the elegant French Suite (around $200) has a king-sized canopied bed with a woodburning fireplace near its foot. A separate sitting room holds a couch.

THE FACTS

Forty-six rooms, most with private baths. Complimentary full breakfast served in the inn's restaurant. Swimming pond. Restaurant and lounge. Disabled access. Closed mid-March through mid-May. Moderate to deluxe.

GETTING THERE

From Interstate 91, take exit 7 (Springfield) and follow Route 11 west through Springfield for approximately eleven miles to Chester. Turn right in Chester, following Route 11 for one-half mile. Turn left on Route 35 and follow south for seven miles to Grafton.

THE OLD TAVERN AT GRAFTON
Route 35 at Route 121 (P.O. Box 9)
Grafton, VT 05146
Telephone toll-free: (800) 843-1801
Web site: www.windham-foundation.org

THE OLD TAVERN AT GRAFTON

Stubborn is the word that aptly describes most everything and everybody in Grafton, a town that has yet to get in step with the rest of the country. It's a community that still whitewashes its picket fences, shingles its bridges, and collects dripping maple sap in buckets.

It's not that time forgot Grafton. It's just that Grafton forgot, or rather refuses, to wind the clock. About the only sign of the modern age is the occasional car that whizzes past the village's quaint namesake tavern hotel.

ROOMS FOR ROMANCE

Don't expect shiny Italian marble, rich window treatments, or bubbling spa tubs at the Old Tavern. What you'll find instead are cozy rooms with comfortable traditional furnishings, a classic beaded rug here and there, and an occasional canopied bed. There are no televisions or telephones. The inn is more charming than luxurious.

Rooms are located not only in the multi-storied and -balconied main building but throughout a variety of nearby village homes.

We spent a night in the main inn, which contains fourteen guest rooms. Those on the third floor that offer large bedrooms and dressing areas are the best bets. Third-floor Rooms 9, 11, 14, and 15 have queen-sized canopy beds.

Among traveling romantics, the most popular room in the main inn is Room 9 (mid $100 range), a third-floor corner that has two double beds and a sitting area furnished with two club-style chairs. The bathroom contains a tub-and-shower combination. We don't recommend the second-floor rooms for a romantic getaway.

The White Gates property is a restored old Grafton home that's now part of the Old Tavern enclave. The first floor has a large living room with a fireplace, a dining room, and a large kitchen with a breakfast nook. The master bedroom has a queen-sized canopied bed and a romantic bathroom with a spa tub and a separate shower. The other two second-floor bedrooms have spa tubs for two and separate showers.

The Old Tavern and several other Grafton buildings are owned and operated by the respected nonprofit Windham Foundation. Rates range from around $200 for a traditional room to $300 or more for a suite.

Windham Hill Inn
311 Lawrence Drive
West Townshend, VT 05359
Telephone: (802) 874-4080;
toll-free: (800) 944-4080
Web site: www.windhamhill.com

THE FACTS

Twenty-one rooms, each with private bath. Complimentary full breakfast served in dining room at tables for two. Restaurant and bar. Heated swimming pool. Tennis court. Hiking trail network. Disabled access. Two-night minimum stay required during weekends and peak foliage season; three-night minimum on certain holiday weekends. Expensive to deluxe.

GETTING THERE

From northbound Interstate 91, take Exit 2 at Brattleboro. Follow "To Route 30" signs into Brattleboro and take Route 30 approximately twenty-three miles northwest to West Townshend. In West Townshend, turn right three tenths of a mile beyond Windham Hill sign and follow for one and a quarter mile to access road on right, just after mailboxes.

WINDHAM HILL INN

Innkeepers Joe and Marina Coneeny can spot them immediately: those visitors who arrive road-weary and tired from daily unpacking and repacking, moving from inn to inn, not wanting to miss out on all that Vermont has to offer. If only they'd made Windham Hill their first stop.

Located conveniently in the heart of southern Vermont, this charming property not only serves up its own impressive dose of Vermont magic, it's also a great central spot from which to take memorable day trips. Communities like Woodstock, Grafton, Williamstown, and Bennington are all within an easy drive.

It was back in 1962 that former owners Hugh and Mary Folsom began welcoming the public to enjoy this enchanting property, then called Windham Hill Farm. One of the projects undertaken by the Folsoms was the construction of an addition that today serves as the Music Room of Windham Hill Inn. Among those who helped in the process was a young summer worker named Will Ackerman, who went on to found the famous Windham Hill Record label.

ROOMS FOR ROMANCE

The guest rooms are contained in two buildings: the Main House and the White Barn. At the rear of the Main House's first level is Tree House (low $300 range), a wonderful space with a cozy window seat, a raised gas stove at the foot of a queen-sized pencil-post bed, and a deck with a view to forever. The Miss Kate Room (mid $200 range), also on this level, has a queen-sized bed, two chairs, and a balcony.

Upstairs are even more romantic accommodations, such as the Jessie Lawrence (around $400), where a large soaking tub presides. This room has a window seat and a king-sized bed. Forget-Me-Not (around $400) also boasts an in-room soaking tub.

In the White Barn, the two of you will enjoy the General Fletcher (low $300 range) with its rustic beamed walls and prominent skylight. This room has a sitting area and a gas stove, and a French door opens to a deck with great views.

We also recommend the Loft Rooms in the White Barn. Among these is Meadowlook (mid $400 range), with its sumptuously canopied and draped king-sized bed, a handsome fieldstone fireplace, expansive windows, and an in-room soaking tub. The Marion Goodfellow (mid $400 range) has a luxurious bathroom with a spa tub for two, as well as an unusual cupola window seat boasting a 360-degree view.

DAYTIME DIVERSIONS

Lake Spofford, just north of Chesterfield Inn in CHESTERFIELD, has boats for rent. In the same region, you can hike in and around Pisgah Park or take a dip in two spring-fed swimming ponds.

BARLETT-bound travelers have convenient access to six downhill ski areas and the dozens of covered bridges of CARROLL COUNTY. The world's oldest cog railway travels to the top of Mount Washington.

Mount Sunapee and Pat's Peak ski areas are within an easy drive of our SUNAPEE region destinations. Snowville visitors have easy access to the outlet shops of NORTH CONWAY.

Summer visitors to Manor on Golden Pond on Squam Lake may catch a sightseeing boat for a tour of sites featured in the acclaimed movie *On Golden Pond.*

TABLES FOR TWO

The majority of our recommended New Hampshire properties have their own dining rooms. In addition to these, we recommend:

T. J. BUCKLEY'S, Brattleboro, VT (Brattleboro is near West Chesterfield, NH)
PETER HAVENS, Brattleboro, VT
THE RARE BEAR, Glen, NH
THOMPSON HOUSE EATERY, Jackson, NH
DANIEL'S RESTAURANT, Henniker, NH
BELLISSIMA TRATTORIA, Newbury Harbor, NH

NEW HAMPSHIRE

THE FACTS

Sixteen rooms, each with private bath; most with wood-burning fireplaces. Complimentary full breakfast. Restaurant offers fixed-price, multicourse meals most nights. Hot tub. Limited disabled access. Two-night minimum stay required most weekends; two- to three-night minimum during foliage season and holiday periods. Expensive to deluxe.

GETTING THERE

From Interstate 93, take exit 35 and follow Route 3 to Route 302. Turn right on Route 302 and drive through White Mountain National Forest for just over seventeen miles to inn on right.

The Notchland Inn
Route 302
Harts Location, Bartlett, NH 03812
Telephone: (603) 374-6131;
toll-free: (800) 866-6131
Web site: www.notchland.com

THE NOTCHLAND INN

A roaring waterfall, long lazy moments of warming sun, a brief mountain drizzle during which a family of moose appeared along the roadside, miles of sweeping ridges ablaze in autumn color—by the time we reached the heart of White Mountain National Forest, Mother Nature had dazzled us with four seasons' worth of magic. Then we rounded a bend at Harts Location and were greeted by a vivid rainbow arcing over the granite façade of the Notchland Inn. "Do you suppose all the guests get this kind of red carpet treatment?" my partner wondered.

We can't guarantee moose or a rainbow, but visitors here can count on spectacular scenery every day of the year and consistent hospitality at one of New Hampshire's most romantic inns.

The Notchland Inn is a handsome, eclectically styled building whose steep roofline is accented with enchanting dormers and gables. The inn sits just off the highway on one hundred acres within a rugged notch of the White Mountains. Mounts Crawford and Hope tower nearby.

During the warmer months, flower and herb gardens add splashes of color to the grounds. Throughout the year, a wooden hot tub awaits in an outdoor gazebo.

ROOMS FOR ROMANCE

Pinkham ($200 range), a front-facing first-floor corner, has windows on three sides. Two wing chairs are set before a woodburning fireplace faced with jade-hued antique tile. The diagonally placed queen-sized bed has an antique Eastlake headboard. The tiny bathroom has a shower stall and the in-room sink is set in an antique dresser.

Carrigain ($200 range) has a queen-sized bed and an oak bureau with a mirror that reflects the fireplace and two blue wing chairs. French doors open to private porches with steps leading into the garden.

On the second floor is Kinsman (mid $200 range), a king-bedded suite where guests can view the fireplace from the sitting room and bedroom, as well as from the soaking tub for two in the bathroom. There's also a steam shower.

Also on the second floor is Crawford ($200 range), a king-bedded corner hideaway sometimes referred to as "the Spy Room." It takes its nickname from a World War II–era guest who spied on passing munitions trains from the tall windows.

New since our first visit are a number of romantic suites, including Carter (mid $200 range), which boasts a stained-glass window, a fireplace, a queen-sized bed, and a spa tub for two. Evans is another premium suite retreat with a furnished deck, a love seat, a fireplace, and a romantic bed placed under a skylight.

THE FACTS

Twenty rooms, each with private bath. Complimentary full breakfast. Restaurant. No disabled access. Two-night minimum stay required during weekends; two- to three-night minimum during holiday periods. Moderate to expensive.

Snowvillage Inn
136 Stewart Road (P.O. Box 68)
Snowville, NH 03832
Telephone: (603) 447-2818
Web site: www.snowvillageinn.com

GETTING THERE

From Interstate 95 at Portsmouth, exit north at the Spaulding Turnpike and follow onto Route 16 north. Exit east on Route 25 at Ossipee and drive to Effingham Falls. Turn left on Route 153 north and follow for ten miles to Eaton and Crystal Lake. At Snowville/Brownfield sign, turn right and follow past beach for one mile to Snowville. Turn right on Stewart Road and follow to inn.

SNOWVILLAGE INN

Distracted by the immediate roadside beauty during our drive up Foss Mountain to Snowvillage Inn, we were momentarily caught off guard by the magnificent view that awaited us at this charming turn-of-the-century former writers' retreat. From the inn's hillside perch, guests are greeted by a seemingly boundless vista that includes the enchanting Presidential Range. In fact, if you make the right reservation, you can wake up to one of New England's more memorable views.

A ten-acre compound under the new ownership of Karen and Bern Galat, the inn comprises twenty rooms spread among three separate buildings: the Chimney House, the Carriage House, and the main inn, which also houses a large and inviting dining room where dinner and breakfast are served daily.

The inn is located approximately six miles from the North Conway outlet stores.

ROOMS FOR ROMANCE

In the main inn, our favorite is queen-bedded Room 14, known as the Robert Frost Room (mid $200 range). This former sun porch on the second floor has an entire wall of windows that overlook the White Mountains. The tiny bathroom has a shower stall. At the time of our most recent travels, Karen and Bern had plans to renovate this and the other main inn rooms.

While they don't offer mountain views, the rooms (mid $200 range) in the Chimney House are among the inn's most romantic. All four of these more contemporary-style rooms have gas fireplaces, queen-sized beds, pine floors and trim, and bathrooms that are a bit larger than those in the other buildings. One of these, Room 16, has a queen-sized canopy bed and offers a pretty view of the adjacent forest. The Chimney House rooms open onto a common room with a couch and a large brick fireplace. The innkeepers promise new luxury suites on the second floor.

At the time of our most recent travels, big plans were also in store for the Carriage House, which was to be rebuilt to offer six suites with spa tubs for two.

THE FACTS

Twenty-five rooms, each with private bath. Complimentary full breakfast served in dining room. Complimentary afternoon refreshments. Restaurant and pub. Spa treatments. Swimming pool. Tennis court. Private Squam Lake beach with canoes and paddle boats. Disabled access. Two-night minimum stay may be required during summer weekends, foliage season, and holiday periods. Expensive to deluxe.

GETTING THERE

From northbound Interstate 93, take exit 24 (Ashland-Holderness). Bear right off exit onto Route 3 south and drive four and seven-tenths miles to inn.

The Manor on Golden Pond
Route 3
Holderness, NH 03245
Telephone: (603) 968-3348;
toll-free: (800) 545-2141
Web site: www.manorongoldenpond.com

THE MANOR ON GOLDEN POND

When seeking a suitably impressive location for the highly acclaimed 1980 movie *On Golden Pond*, starring Henry Fonda and Katherine Hepburn, the filmmakers found a perfect setting in serene Squam Lake, home to the Manor on Golden Pond, our favorite New Hampshire romantic hideaway.

The manor has a romantic history, having been built in 1903 by a well-to-do Englishman for his new wife. Construction took years to complete, and the effort is evident in the meticulous detailing accomplished by craftspeople and artisans who were brought in from around the world to create the expansive lakeview home.

Even the public spaces are equipped for a romantic getaway, offering an intimate dining room, an English-style pub, plenty of places for the two of you to curl up together, and acres of private Squam Lake beachfront.

ROOMS FOR ROMANCE

The majority of guest rooms are found in the stately main house. One of these, Victoria (mid $200 range), is a front-facing room decorated in red and offering a view of the White Mountains and Squam Lake.

The manor's original master bedroom is Buckingham (mid $300 range), whose French doors open to a private deck overlooking the lake and foothills. There's also a fireplace sitting area with a pair of wing chairs.

The Churchill (mid $300 range) is a spectacular corner room with an eye-popping view of the mountains and lake. A blue love seat is placed adjacent to a fireplace, and a circular spa tub for two sits between the bathroom and bedroom. There's also a deck.

Berkshire (mid $300 range) is a spectacular Carriage House room with a circular spa tub for two set in front of a lake- and mountain-view picture window. You'll also enjoy the king-sized canopy bed, the Franklin fireplace, and the balcony.

In the Annexe Chambers, we like the handsome Oxford (high $300 range), with its violet and barn-board walls and Western décor. This room also has a woodburning fireplace, a deck, and a spa tub for two with a view.

Home Hill French Inn and Restaurant
River Road
Plainfield, NH 03781
Telephone: (603) 675-6165
Web site: www.homehillinn.com

THE FACTS

Eleven rooms, each with private bath. Complimentary continental breakfast served at tables for two in the dining room. Restaurant and lounge. Swimming pool. Tennis court. French pétanque court. Free rental bicycles. Fitness facility. Spa treatments. Gift boutique. Disabled access. Two-night minimum stay during special weekends and holiday periods. Deluxe.

GETTING THERE

From Interstate 89, take exit 20 and drive south on Route 12A for three miles. Turn right on River Road and drive three and a half miles to inn's driveway on right.

HOME HILL FRENCH INN AND RESTAURANT

Surrounded by peaceful woods, the nearest town miles behind us, it was easy to imagine our romantic selves transported to France, where hidden country inns like this lure the city-weary with fine food and comfortable accommodations. The fantasy is fueled by a wonderful meal prepared by French innkeeper and executive chef Victoria du Roure, who along with husband Stephane du Roure took ownership of the property in 1997. Prior to the du Roures' ownership, the home had passed through seven generations of the same family over a period of 150 years.

Painted white and accented with contrasting shutters, Home Hill French Inn stands in a clearing near the banks of the Connecticut River, just a few miles north of the longest covered bridge in America. Dartmouth College is nearby.

Of particular note is Home Hill's impressive dining room, boasting dramatic floor-to-ceiling French doors and warm Provençal décor. Victoria, who presides over the kitchen, was classically trained at the Ritz-Escoffier Culinary School at the Ritz Hotel in Paris.

ROOMS FOR ROMANCE

In the main house are four nicely appointed rooms, much upgraded since our initial travels. St. Gaudens is a delightful corner retreat with a queen-sized canopied bed placed between two windows. French and American antiques and a fireplace adorn the room, which looks out over the front and back of the inn.

Maxfield Parrish, also in the main house, is a nice two-room suite consisting of a cozy sitting room with a fireplace and a separate bedroom with another fireplace and a queen-sized bed.

The Carriage House, renovated and expanded since our first visit, has six rooms decorated country French style. Paradou and Barcelonette, both on the second floor, have queen-sized beds and dormer windows. Rates are in the low $400 range for the main house and carriage house rooms.

There's also a delightful private cottage (low $400 range) located near the pool. Called La Piscine, it has a sitting room and a private terrace.

During the wet season, consider a room in the main house so as to avoid a walk through snow or rain to and from the dining room. Carriage House rooms are a wonderful choice during nicer weather.

THE FACTS

Eleven rooms, each with private bath. Complimentary full breakfast served at tables for two. Bar. No disabled access. Two-night minimum stay required during weekends; three-night minimum during some holiday weekends. Moderate to expensive.

GETTING THERE

From Route 91 in Brattleboro, VT, take Route 9 east to Hillsboro, NH. Take Route 202/9 east toward Henniker and Bradford, then Route 114 to Bradford. In Bradford, turn left at junction of Routes 114 and 103. Turn left at next light on Main Street and follow past Town Hall and Bradford Inn. At end of Main Street, curve left (not a sharp left or right) and follow uphill for one and seven-tenths miles to Pleasant View Road on right. Inn is third house on right on Pleasant View Road. For directions from south, please see inn's Web site.

THE ROSEWOOD COUNTRY INN
67 Pleasant View Road
Bradford, NH 03221
Telephone: (603) 938-5253;
toll-free: (800) 938-5273
Web site: www.rosewoodcountryinn.com

THE ROSEWOOD COUNTRY INN

BRADFORD

Because the rates of several of our most highly recommended rooms are beyond the reach of some couples, we occasionally hear from economically minded travelers who are looking for a romantic bargain. At the Rosewood Country Inn, we found a range of accommodations and prices.

Set a comfortable distance from neighbors and town activity, the three-story Rosewood Country Inn reminds us more of a large, comfortable country home than of an inn that's been welcoming visitors since before the turn of the twentieth century. The guest book has been signed by such luminaries as Charlie Chaplin, Jack London, Lillian and Dorothy Gish, and Mary Pickford.

Well maintained and sporting dozens of rose-colored shutters, the inn is decorated with a mix of furnishings that range from antique to traditional. Hand stenciling is featured throughout.

Each morning, guests here are treated to romantic full breakfasts served by candlelight on crystal place settings.

ROOMS FOR ROMANCE

Romantic travelers on a budget will appreciate the cozy Whispering Pines Room (low to mid $100 range) and the Williamsburg Room (mid $100 range), which overlooks the garden and gazebo. Both have queen-sized beds.

The Sturbridge Suite, a large third-floor accommodation with a fireplace and nice windows, was offered at the time of our travels in the high $100 range. The Nathaniel Hawthorne Suite, with its fireplace and spa tub for two, is also a relative bargain at just over $200.

The most coveted room in the inn is the Dreamcatcher Suite (high $200 range), located under the eaves on the third floor, with a delightful window seat with a meadow and mountain view. There's also a king-sized bed, a rustic fireplace, and a sitting area with a couch and chairs. The two of you will also enjoy the corner spa tub for two.

Another inviting window seat is found in the Moondancer Suite (high $100 range), which also has a shower designed for two.

The inn's distinctive turret belongs to the Abigail Adams Suite (low $200 range). There's a queen-sized tester bed with a canopy, and the windowed turret boasts a comfy fainting couch.

THE FACTS

Fifteen rooms, each with private bath; eight with fireplaces. Complimentary full breakfast served at tables for two in the inn's restaurant. Disabled access. Expensive to deluxe.

GETTING THERE

From Interstate 91 in Vermont, take exit 3 north of Brattleboro and follow Route 9 east for two miles over Connecticut River. Turn left on Cross Road, then right into inn's driveway.

CHESTERFIELD INN
Route 9 (P.O. Box 155)
Chesterfield, NH 03443
Telephone: (603) 256-3211;
toll-free: (800) 365-5515
Web site: www.chesterfieldinn.com

CHESTERFIELD INN

Commanding a gentle hillside along a rural highway a couple of miles from the Connecticut River, Chesterfield Inn is difficult to categorize. It's not a country-home-turned-inn; it's not a motel; nor is it a typical hotel, although it has hotel-like interior hallways. It's an appealing century-old hybrid that evolved from diverse stints as a tavern, a farm, and a museum.

With generously sized, well-appointed rooms, interesting exposed beams, balconies, and fireplaces, the property is very well suited to its newest incarnation as a romantic country inn with one of the region's best restaurants.

The community of Chesterfield itself isn't on our list of New England's most romantic destinations, but the inn is definitely worthy of an overnight visit if your itinerary takes you through this lovely region.

ROOMS FOR ROMANCE

Guests may choose from rooms in the main inn building or six newer rooms in the Johanna Wetherby Guest House overlooking either a meadow or a pond.

New since our last visit are two rooms designed with traveling romantics in mind. Room 20 (low $300 range), with its cathedral ceiling, has a king-sized pencil-post bed, two wing chairs set before a gas fireplace, French doors that open to a deck, and a tempting bathroom with a spa tub for two placed in a black tile surround. Room 19 is similarly outfitted. Its bathroom holds a black oval spa tub for two in a white tile surround.

Room 17 (low $200 range) in the main inn, our home for a night, is a bright corner with massive wooden trusses placed above a king-sized bed. Two wing chairs sit in a corner sitting area, and French doors open to your own small balcony offering a view of the sunset and the hills through trees. The large bathroom is equipped with a tub-and-shower combination.

Another of our favorites is Room 18 (low $200 range) in the main inn, where weathered barn wood has been incorporated into the fireplace wall and beamed ceiling. This corner room has a king-sized bed, a gas fireplace, a large bathroom with a tub-and-shower combination, and a view of the Vermont hills.

Room 11 faces the entry walkway and consequently isn't completely private unless the drapes are drawn. Room 10 (low $200 range), the honeymoon suite on the ground floor, has a spa tub for two and a fireplace. However, its front-facing view is also not completely private.

In the guest cottage, Rooms 21 and 24 (low $200 range) are our favorites.

DAYTIME DIVERSIONS

Summer in the Berkshires means theater and music, and options range from the Stockbridge Cabaret and Tanglewood Music Festival in LENOX to the popular Berkshire Theatre Festival in STOCKBRIDGE. The Norman Rockwell Museum is on Main Street in Stockbridge.

The famous Salem Wax Museum, at 288 Derby Street in SALEM, is only a short distance from our Cape Ann destinations.

In ROCKPORT, you can see the sights by taking a walking tour (ask your innkeeper for a map) or by catching a Cape Ann Tours trolley car. The village shops in Rockport will keep you busy for hours.

On MARTHA'S VINEYARD, the red and orange cliffs at Gay Head are among the most popular destinations among island-combers. Bicycling is also big on the Vineyard, where cycle paths run along the ocean between Oak Bluffs and Edgartown. Ask your innkeeper for locations of rental shops and inspiring routes.

In BOSTON, book-lovers should be sure to visit Trident Booksellers and Café on fashionable Newbury Street. Clear Flour Bakery on Thorndike Street in Brookline, supplies the breads for a number of great Boston restaurants and also operates a popular retail outlet.

A multi-image production about life on NANTUCKET by island resident Cary Hazlegrove (who created the photos for this book) is shown daily during the summer months in the Methodist Church on Centre Street. Call (508) 228-3783.

TABLES FOR TWO

BISTRO ZINC, Lenox
PEARL'S, Great Barrington
ONCE UPON A TABLE, Stockbridge
SWEET BASIL GRILL, South Lee
PELLINO'S, Marblehead
JACK TAR, Marblehead
DAILY CATCH (for seafood), Boston
TURNER FISHERIES (for chowder), Boston

MASSACHUSETTS

THE FACTS

Five rooms, each with private bath. Complimentary full breakfast served at communal table. Complimentary afternoon refreshments. Guest computer with Internet access. Disabled access. Three-night minimum stay during July and August. Deluxe.

GETTING THERE

From the Massachusetts Turnpike (Interstate 90), take exit 2 and bear right onto Route 20 west. Follow through Lee (Route 20 makes a right turn in Lee) for approximately four miles. After Cranwell on right, turn left at stoplight on Walker Street. Follow Walker Street into Lenox Village, staying left of monument and heading downhill for approximately one and a half miles. At Tanglewood main gate, turn right on Under Mountain Road and follow for seven-tenths of a mile to inn on left.

STONOVER FARM
169 Under Mountain Road
Lenox, MA 01240
Telephone: (413) 637-9100
Web site: www.stonoverfarm.com

STONOVER FARM

It's a long way from producing gold records by the likes of Cheap Trick and Ted Nugent in Los Angeles to running a small bed-and-breakfast inn in the Berkshires. However, proprietor Tom Werman has struck gold yet again with Stonover Farm, a luxury hideaway that might just turn out to be his greatest hit ever.

Tom and his wife, Suky, a former teacher, stumbled on the bucolic farmstead a few years ago after the nation's musical tastes changed and Tom grew weary of "the business." They sold their L.A. home and a vacation place in Nantucket and settled in Lenox, rehabbing the 1890 farmhouse and restoring the beautiful grounds. Their first guest was Linda Ronstadt, who happened to be headlining at Tanglewood, a fifteen-minute walk away.

ROOMS FOR ROMANCE

Stonover Farm has only five guest accommodations, so the two of you won't be sharing this idyllic property with many others. For the ultimate in intimate privacy, we recommend Rock Cottage (around $500), a freestanding hideaway on a hill with a view of the duck pond. The living area is furnished with a couch and chairs set before a stone fireplace and an entertainment center. There's also a dining area and a fresh, bright, nicely windowed kitchen. Laundry facilities are found in the basement. The master bedroom has a king-sized bed, and there's a sleeping turret upstairs with two additional beds.

Suite One (mid $300 range) spans a large section of the inn's second floor and includes a cozy sitting room, a bedroom with a woodsy view, and a bathroom that's a romantic haven, equipped with a shower designed for two, a soaking tub for two, and a double vanity.

The largest accommodation is Suite 2 (mid $300 range), a nicely equipped accommodation with a sitting room furnished with a sofa and armchair, a bedroom with multiple windows, a Heatilator fireplace, and a bathroom with a spa tub and separate shower.

Suite 3 (mid $300 range) has an inviting window seat at the foot of a king-sized bed and a sitting room where a small sofa and rocker face a beautiful Palladian window. A tiled shower built for two is found in the bathroom.

Blantyre
16 Blantyre Road
Lenox, MA 01240
Telephone: (413) 637-3556
Web site: www.blantyre.com

THE FACTS

Twenty-five rooms, suites, and cottages, each with private bath; six with woodburning fireplaces; one with wood stove. Complimentary continental breakfast served at tables for two or in your room. Restaurant, heated swimming pool, sauna, spa, tennis courts, and croquet lawns. Disabled access. Two-night minimum stay required during weekends and holiday periods. Deluxe.

GETTING THERE

From the Massachusetts Turnpike (Interstate 90), take Route 20 at Lee (exit 2) and turn right onto Route 20 west. Follow for three miles and turn right on Blantyre Road. The inn is approximately two hours from Boston and just under three hours from New York.

BLANTYRE

A gated twenty-five-acre country estate, Blantyre is easily the most exclusive of our fifty romantic New England destinations. Travelers who enjoy formal elegance and being pampered in exquisite accommodations will feel quite comfortable in this magnificent Scottish-style manor.

Originally a private summer retreat, the turn-of-the-century property was restored by Senator John Fitzpatrick and his wife, Ann, during the 1980s and opened as an upscale inn.

The baronial public rooms of the main house are reminiscent of a royal palace. The priceless antique furnishings, museum-quality tapestries, ornately carved wooden ceilings and walls, and leaded glass windows are awe-inspiring.

Fixed-price meals (jacket and tie required) are served in a beautiful octagon-shaped dining room with fabric-covered walls.

ROOMS FOR ROMANCE

The eight guest rooms in the main house contain many of the same elegant trappings found in the public spaces. One of our romantic favorites is the elegant Laurel Suite (mid $700 range), in which a queen-sized four-poster bed is placed in a draped bay window. This exquisitely decorated room also has a woodburning fireplace and a sitting area with a couch and cushy chairs.

Less expensive are the pretty Ribbon Room, with a king-sized bed and overstuffed love seat; the Bouquet Room with a queen-sized bed; and the somewhat whimsical Toile Room, a small hideaway with a queen-sized bed set behind an arched entryway. Each is available in the $500 range.

We prefer the rhapsodic environs of the turreted main house, but Blantyre does offer other options that include a collection of rooms in a remote two-story carriage house and cottages.

New since our first visit is the ultra-romantic and impressive Ice House Suite (around $1,000), which comprises the upper level of the Ice House Cottage. This exclusive hideaway has an enclosed porch, a living room, a cozy window seat, and a spa tub for two.

Fernbrook, on the second floor of the carriage house, is a romantic two-level room with a small balcony. The lower level is a large sitting room with a couch, a chair, and a table and chairs set; the loft, with a king-sized bed, is accessed by an iron stairway. Carriage-house rooms range from the mid $400 range to the mid $500 range.

We were also impressed with River View (mid $700 range), with its king-sized bed, two fireplaces, a veranda, a separate sitting room and bedroom, and a bathroom with a shower.

THE FACTS

Ten rooms, each with private bath. Complimentary full breakfast served in dining room at tables for two. No disabled access. Two-night minimum stay required during weekends; three-night minimum during summer months and holiday periods. Moderate to expensive.

GETTING THERE

From the Massachusetts Turnpike (Interstate 90), take exit 2 (Lee) and follow signs for Route 120 west toward Stockbridge. Follow Route 120 for three miles to inn on left.

HISTORIC MERRELL INN
1565 Pleasant Street
South Lee, MA 01260
Telephone: (413) 243-1794;
toll-free: (800) 243-1794
Web site: www.merrell-tavern.com

HISTORIC MERRELL INN

When we learned in advance of our visit that Historic Merrell Inn was built while George Washington was president, our first visions were of chamber pots, candles, and drafty rooms. Instead, we were greeted by a stylishly enchanting environment with fully equipped private bathrooms, queen-sized canopied beds, smart décor, romantic lighting, and innkeepers committed to a comfortable blend of old and new.

A national heirloom built around 1794, the building originally functioned as a residence but has served as a tavern and inn for many generations. Still in place are a number of antique fixtures, including what is believed to be the nation's only remaining birdcage-style bar, through which spirits and ales have undoubtedly been liberally dispensed over the years. Fireplaces that warm the public and guest rooms are also original to the building, and many of the inn's antique furnishings date from the 1790s.

ROOMS FOR ROMANCE

We have favorites on each of the three floors. On the first level, Room 1 (high $100 range), originally the inn's parlor, is among the larger rooms and boasts a woodburning fireplace and a queen-sized canopy bed.

On the second floor, Rooms 2 and 9 (high $100 range) also have fireplaces. Room 9 is a corner room with pine floors and a gold velour love seat.

Tastefully painted deep purple walls await behind the door of Room 7 (high $100 range) on the third floor. This corner room is furnished with a king-sized bed and handsome antiques. The wall-papered bathroom has a shower stall. We found Rooms 5 and 10 (high $100 range) to be a bit small.

Room 6 (high $100 range), ours for a night, is situated on the third floor, carved from space that originally served as a ballroom. Rose designs on the spread of the queen-sized bed are carried through to window hangings and the wallpaper border, as well as to the bed linens.

New since our first visit is the River View Suite (high $200 range), the inn's premier accommodation. Located in a separate wing overlooking the Housatonic River and the perennial gardens, the comfortable suite has a private balcony, lots of windows, a sitting room, and a king-sized bed facing a wall of bookshelves and a fireplace. The bathroom has a tub-and-shower combination.

THE FACTS

Eleven rooms, each with private bath. Complimentary full breakfast served at small tables in candlelit dining room; complimentary afternoon and evening refreshments. Swimming pool. Golf course and tennis courts across the street. Free bicycle rentals. Two-night minimum stay required on weekends in June, September, and October; three-night minimum on weekends during July and August and on three-day holiday weekends. Moderate to deluxe.

GETTING THERE

From Massachusetts Turnpike (Interstate 90), take exit 2 (Lee). Turn right off exit ramp on Route 20 to Lee. Go straight at stop sign in Lee (despite Route 20's right turn) and follow one-half mile to inn on left.

APPLEGATE INN

It's hard to believe that once upon a time, this gracious 1920s-era Georgian colonial mansion, which presides over a manicured estate of six acres, was used only as a summer residence by its owner, a successful New York surgeon.

Beyond the circular entry and dramatic columned porte cochere, the stately home proves to be as impressive inside as it is from the outside. It retains a regal elegance while welcoming today's discerning guests with all of the modern romantic flourishes we could hope for. This is one destination that has no doubt improved with age—and obviously a great deal of care.

The property is only a half mile from the charming town of Lee and directly across the street from a country club with a golf course and tennis courts that are open to the public. Stockbridge and Tanglewood are nearby.

ROOMS FOR ROMANCE

There are eight enchanting rooms in the main residence, each one uniquely styled and furnished. At the top of our Most Romantic list are Rooms 7 and 8, known as the Sky View Suites (mid $300 range). In Room 7, there's a king-sized bed, a fireplace, and an old-fashioned soaking tub placed next to a window and looking out over trees and lawn.

Arguably nicer is Room 8, which boasts an oversized marble bath with a spa tub for two. Both rooms have balconies and king-sized beds.

Room 1 (mid $300 range) is a graceful and stylish corner room, decorated in green tones and furnished with a sofa and a pair of wing chairs placed under a window.

Room 3 (mid $200 range) holds a queen-sized sleigh bed. This is a bright, nicely wallpapered room with two wing chairs placed in a corner adjacent to a fireplace. Room 5 (mid $200 range) boasts a queen-sized bed draped with a gauzy canopy.

The estate's former Carriage House is now home to Room 10 (mid $300 range), a suitably romantic suite with a king-sized bronze bed, a love seat, a fireplace, a wet bar, a spa tub for two, and a private patio.

APPLEGATE INN
279 West Park Street
Lee, MA 01238
Telephone: (413) 243-4451;
toll-free: (800) 691-9012
Web site: www.applegateinn.com

Yankee Clipper Inn
96 Granite Street
Rockport, MA 01966
Telephone: (508) 546-3407;
toll-free: (800) 545-3699
Web site: www.yankeeclipperinn.com

THE FACTS

Sixteen rooms, each with private bath. Complimentary breakfast buffet. Restaurant serves English-style afternoon tea and dinner depending on season. Heated swimming pool. No disabled access. Two-night minimum stay required during weekends; three-night minimum during holiday periods. Call for winter availability. Expensive to deluxe.

GETTING THERE

From Greater Boston, follow Route 128 north to Cape Ann, passing through two traffic circles in Gloucester. Continue on Route 128 to its end. At first set of traffic lights, turn left onto Route 127. Drive approximately three miles to where highway makes a sharp left turn, and follow sign toward Pigeon Cove, one and two-tenths miles to inn.

YANKEE CLIPPER INN

If you were to ask a typical American traveler to name a romantic New England coastal getaway destination that's within a short drive of Boston, chances are the answer would be Cape Cod. Put the same question to a Bostonian in-the-know, and the whispered response is more likely to be Cape Ann.

Long a favorite destination among Bay State residents, Rockport and Cape Ann's other enchanting towns have never quite achieved the mythical status of those on the world-famous cape to the south. However, they remain some of New England's most shimmering jewels.

Commanding a gentle ocean-view knoll at the rocky edge of the Atlantic, Yankee Clipper Inn represents some of the best of Cape Ann. It's conveniently close to the inviting shops of Rockport but is set in a quiet residential area of town.

The Yankee Clipper compound consists of the main inn building, an eclectically designed seaside mansion set just yards from the surf. The inn's restaurant, common areas, and several guest rooms are located here. A stone path leads to the Quarterdeck, a three-story ocean-front structure built in the 1960s and boasting panoramic Atlantic vistas. Since our first visit, bathrooms in this building have been upgraded, and most rooms have been outfitted with single-sized spa tubs.

ROOMS FOR ROMANCE

We stayed in freshly spruced-up Room 37 (mid $300 range) on the ground floor of the Quarterdeck, which contains comfortable deep-cushioned wicker chairs and a king-sized bed. Through our large picture window, we watched the ocean turn from a sparkling late-afternoon blue to a seductive dusky black. Our Quarterdeck favorites are those on the second and third floors, where you'll be able to savor the ocean view through open drapes without compromising your privacy.

In the inn building, there are eight attractive guest rooms. John and Jacqueline Kennedy spent the night in Room 24 during a campaign trip in 1959. Offered in the low $200 range, this is a spacious corner suite with a king-sized bed, a comfy chaise, built-in bookshelves, and a private sun porch whose seven windows boast an expansive ocean view.

Rooms 27 and 31 (high $300 range) have private decks, and Room 23 (high $300 range) has its own enclosed glass porch.

THE FACTS

Twenty-one rooms, each with private bath. Complimentary continental breakfast buffet served in dining room at tables for two or four. Complimentary afternoon refreshments. Swimming pool. No disabled access. Two-night minimum stay required during weekends; three-night minimum during holiday and high-season weekends. Expensive to deluxe.

GETTING THERE

From Interstate 95, follow Route 114 east to Salem-Marblehead, where it becomes Pleasant Street. Follow Pleasant Street to end and turn left onto Washington Street. Follow two blocks to inn on right. From Boston, follow Route 1A north to Route 129 east. In Marblehead, follow Atlantic Avenue and take first right turn after filling station onto Washington Street. Follow one-quarter mile to inn on right. Parking is behind inn.

HARBOR LIGHT INN
58 Washington Street
Marblehead, MA 01945
Telephone: (781) 631-2186
Web site: www.harborlightinn.com

HARBOR LIGHT INN

Marblehead is less than twenty miles from the high-rises of cosmopolitan Boston, but the roots of this historic village are still firmly planted in the eighteenth century. Among the intriguing old façades facing narrow Washington Street in the town's historic section are those of Harbor Light Inn, created through the union of two venerable homes constructed in the early 1700s.

Although the Harbor Light is our oldest romantic New England getaway destination, its age is quite deceiving. Sure, there are the requisite trappings of another time, such as fine woodwork, brass trim, and masonry, as well as the occasional creaky floorboard. But the inn's operators have taken great pains to provide contemporary comforts, like spa tubs for two in several rooms. There's even a swimming pool hidden in the rear courtyard.

ROOMS FOR ROMANCE

Room 22 (around $300) is the most popular, primarily because of the raised spa tub for two that sits surrounded by green plants under a skylight in the mirrored bathroom. The bedroom holds a queen-sized canopied bed and a working fireplace.

During the summer months, Room 4 (mid $200 range) at the rear of the inn is a favorite, especially for its private outdoor deck. This room has a queen-sized four-poster bed, a love seat, and pine furniture. The small bathroom holds a square spa tub for two.

Decorated in rich red tones, Room 5 (mid $200 range) is a remote front-facing corner on the first floor. In addition to a handsome carved queen-sized canopy bed, this room holds a built-in settee, two wing chairs, a fireplace, and a rug-covered oak floor. There's a six-foot-long spa tub for two set under a glass-block window in the bathroom.

Room 6 (mid $200 range), which faces the inn's rear courtyard, has a fireplace with an original bread oven. This room also has a spa tub for two.

All the guest rooms on the third floor have dark, rough-hewn, exposed-beam ceilings. One of these, Room 32 (around $200), is an attractive three-windowed corner with cathedral ceilings, a brick fireplace, bookshelves, and a queen-sized four-poster bed. The tiled bathroom has a tub-and-shower combination.

THE FACTS

Nine rooms, each with private bath, fireplace, spa tub for two, and CD and videocassette player. Complimentary continental breakfast served in your room. CD and videocassette library. DSL Internet service. Disabled access. Elevator. Two-night minimum stay required during weekends and holiday periods. Deluxe.

GETTING THERE

Inn is located in Beacon Hill district, north of Boston Common, on Charles Street, between Pinckney and Mount Vernon Streets. From Interstate 93, exit at Storrow Drive. Move to left lane and take first exit off Storrow Drive (labeled Government Center). Turn right at the stoplight on Charles Street and follow for two and a half blocks to inn on right.

THE CHARLES STREET INN

Reportedly America's first model home when it was built in 1860, the Charles Street Inn has been transformed into a model inn, providing traveling romantics with a luxurious boutique alternative to Boston's high-rise hotels.

The distinctive brick townhouse served for years as an apartment complex until new owners essentially gutted the interior in 1999. What resulted is an impressive, finely appointed inn that combines tasteful Victoriana with contemporary comforts like spa tubs, granite counters, and even high-speed Internet service.

ROOMS FOR ROMANCE

The two of you can't go wrong with any of the nine rooms, but we have our own favorites. For example, the Henry James Room (low $400 range) makes an elegant statement with its king-sized canopied bed, tones of greens and golds, rich drapes, a comfortable couch at the foot of the bed, a marble fireplace, and stately American and Spanish furnishings.

The Oliver Wendell Holmes Room (around $400), which looks into the treetops overlooking Mount Vernon Square Park, is furnished with an impressive king-sized sleigh bed and two chairs, but no couch.

The coral-toned Isabella Stewart Gardner Room (around $400) boasts a fresh, feminine look with its partially canopied king-sized bed, brass chandelier, antique art, couch, and small desk placed in a bay window. This room, which faces Charles Street, is a favorite of honeymooners and couples celebrating a special occasion.

The Louisa May Alcott Room (mid $300 range) has a fainting couch, a nice sweep of windows overlooking the rooftops of Beacon Hill, and a painted queen-sized iron and brass bed. Facing Charles Street, the Edith Wharton Room (around $400) has a sunny bay window furnished with a comfy settee, a queen-sized bed, and matching hand-carved French armoires.

THE CHARLES STREET INN
94 Charles Street
Boston, MA 02114
Telephone: (617) 314-8900;
toll-free: (877) 772-8900
Web site: www.charlesstreetinn.com

THE FACTS

Three hundred thirty-five rooms, each with private bath and balcony or terrace. Four restaurants, bar, room service, and concierge. Resort shuttle. Private beach. Two heated indoor pools and four outdoor pools. Fitness facility. Family activities. Cycling trails and bicycle rentals. Eighteen-hole golf course. Tennis complex. Disabled access. Deluxe.

GETTING THERE

Located on Route 6A (Old King's Highway), in Brewster, at the south end of Cape Cod. Resort is approximately ninety miles from Boston's Logan Airport.

OCEAN EDGE RESORT AND GOLF CLUB
Route 6A
2907 Main Street
Brewster, MA 02631
Telephone: (508) 896-9000;
toll-free: (800) 343-6074
Web site: www.oceanedge.com

OCEAN EDGE RESORT AND GOLF CLUB

One of the premier seaside resorts on Cape Cod, Ocean Edge Resort and Golf Club is a perfect destination for couples who enjoy a variety of activities in an exclusive and pampering environment. Name the activity —from golf and tennis to yoga and spin classes—and Ocean Edge delivers. The resort even boasts a precious stretch of private Cape Cod beachfront.

Although it's one of our top romantic getaway picks, Ocean Edge is probably best suited for a book called *Weeks for Two,* since a single weekend won't allow you to sufficiently experience all that this four-hundred-acre resort has to offer. And with a resort shuttle and four restaurants, you'd never need to leave the grounds.

Ocean Edge traces its roots to the late 1800s, when Samuel Mayo Nickerson and his wife, Matilda, constructed a lavish summer estate and a private game preserve here. The original fairytale mansion burned in 1906 and was replaced by the grand country estate that now serves as the resort's centerpiece. Today, Ocean Edge is an exclusive membership club that's also open to guests.

ROOMS FOR ROMANCE

Ocean Edge has 335 accommodations in all. These include eighty-eight hotel rooms (starting in the mid $300 range) and hundreds of one-, two-, and three-bedroom villas.

At the time of our travels, Ocean Edge was emerging from a multiyear, multimillion-dollar renovation that included improvements to the resort's varied accommodations and the addition of wireless Internet access.

The Bay Pines Villas, which have been refurnished, are situated a short walk from the private beach. These units, which carry weekly tariffs starting in the mid $4,000 range, boast two and three bedrooms and are equipped with kitchens, washers and dryers, dining rooms, and living rooms.

The Britterige Villas are surrounded by golf course fairways near the outdoor pools. The Arbor Villas, added in 2001, overlook the golf course and have kitchens and patios.

THE FACTS

Sixteen rooms, each with private bath and fireplace. Complimentary full breakfast served at tables for two and four or in your room. Complimentary morning coffee and newspaper. Complimentary afternoon tea and refreshments. Complimentary snack basket. Disabled access. Three-night minimum stay required during high season and holiday periods. Moderate to deluxe.

GETTING THERE

From Route 6 on Cape Cod, take Route 137 to exit 11 (Chatham). Drive south to Route 28 and turn left. At Chatham Center, follow traffic circle out of town on Route 28 toward Orleans. Follow Route 28/Old Harbor Road for approximately one-half mile to inn on left.

THE CAPTAIN'S HOUSE INN
369–377 Old Harbor Road
Chatham, MA 02633
Telephone: (508) 945-0127
Web site: www.captainshouseinn.com

THE CAPTAIN'S HOUSE INN

It's unlikely that even Captain Hiram Harding, the privileged skipper who commissioned this patrician home, savored the romantic opulence available to guests today. It's more than a century and a half old, but there's little doubt that the Captain's House Inn is in finer shape today than the day it was completed.

Regarded consistently by respected lodging reviewers as the Cape's best-run hostelry, the inn owes its high standing to proprietors Dave and Jan McMaster, who continue to bestow loving attention on the gorgeous two-and-a-half-acre grounds and the charming vintage buildings.

Proprietors of the Captain's House Inn since 1993, the McMasters previously operated a B&B and pub near Oxford, England. In fact, the couple was drawn here by similarities between Chatham and Britain's small villages. Jan is a native of England, and Dave is a retired Navy commander and the founder and former chief executive of a computer company.

Guest accommodations at the Captain's House are spread among a main house, the vintage Captain's Cottage, the Carriage House, and the more recently constructed "Stables." The rooms are named after the daughters of Captain Hiram, as well as for some of the ships he sailed.

ROOMS FOR ROMANCE

In the main house, the intimate and elegant second-floor Eliza Jane Suite (low $300 range) has a fireplace visible from the small seating area as well as from the queen-sized four-poster bed. The bathroom has a corner spa tub for two and a separate shower.

Panoramic views through three walls of windows make the Clarissa Suite (low $400 range) a popular romantic retreat. Strategically located to take advantage of the views is a king-sized four-poster bed, while the sitting room holds a pair of comfortable chairs facing a cozy fireplace flanked by windows. There's a spa tub for two and a separate room with a shower for two.

Lady Mariah (mid $300 range) is a gorgeous Captain's Cottage room whose decadent bathroom with a spa tub for two and a fireplace makes this a popular choice for honeymooners.

For the ultimate romantic getaway experience we recommend the Lydia Harding Suite (mid $400 range), a huge accommodation boasting a living room with multiple sitting areas, a spacious balcony, and a bedroom with a king-sized four-poster bed. There's also a spa tub for two and a romantic shower for two.

THE FACTS

Six rooms, each with private bath; six with woodburning fireplaces. Complimentary full breakfast served at tables for two. Swimming pool and tennis court. Beach passes. Disabled access. Two-night minimum stay required during weekends and holiday periods. Expensive to deluxe.

GETTING THERE

Inn is located off Highway 28A and Blacksmith Shop Road in West Falmouth. Innkeepers will provide specific driving instructions after confirming reservations.

THE INN AT WEST FALMOUTH

WEST FALMOUTH

Even in a locale as famous and well traveled as Cape Cod, a few secrets remain. The Inn at West Falmouth, which lies hidden and unmarked at the end of a narrow wooded gravel lane well off the beaten path, is quite possibly the cape's most romantic destination. A shingled home that oozes classic nineteenth-century New England charm, the inn is located only about fifteen minutes from the Woods Hole ferry terminal. As such, it's a perfect resting place for Martha's Vineyard–bound travelers, as well as for those simply in the mood for a relaxing Cape Cod getaway.

When we first discovered this delightful hideaway, the former summer cottage had recently been rescued from years of neglect. Walls were removed to create a collection of stunning suites and rooms with spacious Italian marble–floored bathrooms and intriguing windows and cozy balconies. Some rooms offer splendid views of Buzzards Bay and the ocean, just a half mile away. A small swimming pool and a tennis court are the crowning touches.

ROOMS FOR ROMANCE

Guest quarters exude a romantically eclectic aura. Your room might combine colorful chintz with an antique Oriental chest or a Moroccan rug with luxurious Waverly fabric. Many guests find that the spa tubs will hold two friendly people.

We spent an enchanting summer night in Room 3 (high $300 range), a spacious suite featuring a sitting nook with cushioned window seat, a fireplace, a canopied four-poster queen-sized bed, and a large pool- and bay-view balcony with a comfortable chaise-and-chair set.

Room 6 (high $300 range) is a private second-floor corner hideaway with a canopied queen-sized bed, a fireplace, a leather chaise, and a tiny bay-view balcony with a table and chairs.

Decorated in yellow tones with an English theme, Room 5 (mid $200) has a fireplace and offers a nice wooded view. A favorite honeymoon hideaway, Room 1 (low $300 range), boasts a great ocean view, romantic sunsets, a tiny Juliet balcony, and a skylit bathroom with a spa tub.

THE INN AT WEST FALMOUTH
P.O. Box 1208
West Falmouth, MA 02574
Telphone: (508) 540-7696
Web site: www.innatwestfalmouth.com

THE FACTS

Twenty-three rooms, each with private bath. Complimentary continental breakfast included in rate; full breakfast available at additional charge. L'Etoile restaurant. Disabled access. Two-night minimum stay required during most weekends in season; three-night minimum during holiday periods. Deluxe.

GETTING THERE

From Oak Bluffs ferry dock, drive south on Seaview Avenue, which becomes Beach Road, then Edgartown-Oak Bluffs Road, and finally Main Street in Edgartown. Turn right on Summer Street and follow to inn on left. For ferry reservations, contact Steamship Authority at (508) 477-8600.

THE CHARLOTTE INN
27 South Summer Street (P.O. Box 2280)
Edgartown, MA 02539
Telephone: (508) 627-4151
Web site: www.relaischateaux.com/charlotte

THE CHARLOTTE INN

In our Vineyard wanderings, we've failed to discover a more enchanting community than Edgartown. And we can't imagine a finer romantic complement to an overnight Edgartown visit than a guest room at this sublime inn.

Set at the heart of town and spread among a collection of fine buildings that run from patrician to quaint, the inn is well positioned for tours not only of Edgartown but also the island. It's also a short walk to the harbor and the Chappaquiddick ferry.

The compound's centerpiece is a mid-nineteenth-century whaling merchant's home. The lower level holds the registration area, grand parlors, and an open and airy dining room. Winding walkways, hidden gardens, and patios offer visiting couples lots of opportunities for private outdoor enjoyment.

While a few guests have described attitudes at this luxury inn as somewhat smug, the majority of reports have been quite positive, and many were effusive.

ROOMS FOR ROMANCE

Of the rooms in the main house, Room 12 (mid $500 range) is one of our top recommendations for a romantic getaway. Features include a canopied four-poster bed, a woodburning fireplace, and a separate sitting area. Rooms 9 and 10 (around $300) are among the inn's less expensive accommodations. These smaller rooms have double beds. You'll need to invest at least $325 for a room with a queen-sized bed.

Next door is Summer House, the former residence of a sea captain that now houses seven guest rooms. The lower-level rooms face a long covered porch overlooking an exquisitely sculpted lawn and garden area. Room 14 (mid $700 range) has a fireplace, a sitting area, and a grand piano.

At the rear of the property stands a two-story refurbished carriage house whose rooms are among the inn's most secluded. Room 2 (from around $500) is a small, handsome hideaway with deep green carpeting, English antiques, a queen-sized four-poster bed, and a love seat. It also boasts a private lawn and garden area.

Directly across the tree-lined street from the main building is Garden House, which dates from 1705. There are a handful of comfortable rooms here. Room 20, priced at around $300, is the least expensive.

High-season rates (from early June through October) at the Charlotte Inn are among the island's most expensive. However, nightly rates at other times of the year are as much as $100 less.

Visitors should be aware that traffic can be a problem in Edgartown, and guests may have to park a few blocks away from the inn.

THE FACTS

Fourteen rooms, each with private bath. Complimentary full breakfast served at tables for two or more. Complimentary continental breakfast can be delivered to your room. No disabled access. Two-night minimum stay required during weekends, three-night minimum during holiday periods. Expensive to deluxe.

GETTING THERE

From Vineyard Haven ferry dock, turn right at stop sign and turn right on Main Street. Drive one mile to inn on left. From Oak Bluffs ferry dock, follow signs to Vineyard Haven and turn right on Main Street. Drive one mile to inn on left. For ferry reservations, contact Steamship Authority at (508) 477-8600.

THORNCROFT INN
460 Main Street
Vineyard Haven, MA 02568-1022
Telephone: (508) 693-3333;
toll-free: (800) 332-1236
Web site: www.thorncroftinn.com

THORNCROFT INN

VINEYARD HAVEN, MARTHA'S VINEYARD

On this romantic island that appears to have been created especially for lovers, there's a seemingly endless list of places to go and things to see and do together. Therein lies the essence of what we call the Thorncroft dilemma. This lovely inn is almost too difficult to leave, even for a few hours of Vineyard exploration.

Not only do we rank Thorncroft Inn as the island's preeminent lodging choice, we consider it one of the finest and most romantic destinations in all of New England.

ROOMS FOR ROMANCE

One of the most romantic features we've yet discovered in our travels is found in both Rooms 1 and 10 (high $400 range). Guests here are treated to hot tubs that are so big they're housed in completely private adjoining rooms. Room 1 is tastefully wallpapered and holds a beautiful custom-built antique queen-sized bed and a fireplace. A queen-sized canopied bed that's over two hundred years old is the centerpiece of Room 10, which has a fireplace, a sitting area, and a private entry.

Romantic warm-water experiences are also available in Rooms 9 and 14 (mid $400 range), where spacious spa tubs for two are placed in mirrored bedroom alcoves.

Our generous slice of heaven for a night was Room 12 (high $300 range) on the second floor of the remote Carriage House. This hideaway, which has windows on three sides, is reached by a lighted gravel path through a dense growth of trees and brush at the rear of the property. The centerpiece of this large corner room is a raised queen-sized bed with a fishnet canopy. A wood fire is laid in the marble fireplace and awaits only a match. French doors open onto a private balcony with chairs overlooking a side lawn. The bath is compact, holding a tub-and-shower combination.

At the time of our most recent travels, the inn offered several rooms for around $300. One of the best is Room 7 on the second floor of the main building. It's furnished with a romantic queen-sized canopied bed and has a pair of chairs. The bathroom has a tub-and-shower combination.

THE FACTS

Thirty-five rooms and cottages, each with private bath. Complimentary morning coffee, tea, and pastries. Complimentary afternoon refreshments. Restaurant. Beach towels and lounge chairs. Complimentary mountain bicycle rentals. Tennis courts. Spa treatments. Croquet. Numerous summer activities, such as tours, sailing, and kayaking, included in room rate. Movies delivered to your room with popcorn. The Wauwinet is closed during the winter. Visit inn's Web site for dates. Deluxe.

GETTING THERE

The Wauwinet is located at the end of Wauwinet Road, nine miles from Nantucket town. The inn will arrange transportation for those traveling to Nantucket via Hy-Line Cruises' fast ferry.

THE WAUWINET

After twenty years of wonderful vacations on Nantucket, Bostonians Stephen and Jill Karp decided to make a permanent investment in the island. So they purchased the historic and somewhat tired Wauwinet and invested $8 million in a renovation that lasted nearly two years. Now, nearly twenty years later, the inn has earned a worldwide reputation as Nantucket's preeminent destination.

Set at the end of a road on a spit of land surrounded by water, the Wauwinet is the only place to stay on the island where one can enjoy beaches on both the frothy surf of the Atlantic and the calm, warmer waters of Nantucket Bay. Set a comfortable distance from bustling Nantucket town, the resort enjoys a heavenly location that combines rolling dunes, romantic pathways, expanses of lawn, and gardens. A wildlife preserve borders the property.

ROOMS FOR ROMANCE

"Casual country coastal" might be an apt description of the Wauwinet's delightful, unpretentious guest-room décor. "Varied" is how we'd describe the menu of rooms. Some guests report having being unpleasantly surprised by the small size of the resort's standard bedrooms and bathrooms ($500–$700 range) on the second and third floors of the inn. These rooms, which do not offer bay views, are indeed cozy.

Those who like to spread out would be advised to upgrade to a "superior bedroom" (around $800), which includes a nice sitting area with oversized chairs but no view to speak of. Deluxe versions of this room offering Nantucket Bay views carry nightly rates approaching $1,000.

THE WAUWINET
P.O. Box 2580
Nantucket, MA 02584
Telephone: (508) 228-0145;
toll-free: (800) 426-8718
Web site: www.wauwinet.com

THE FACTS

Twenty-eight rooms, suites, and cottages, each with private bath. Complimentary continental breakfast served in lobby or in your room. Restaurant. Swimming pool. Massage therapy. Steam rooms and spas. Private swimming beach with umbrellas, chairs, and towels. Exercise room. No disabled access. Four-night minimum stay during high season only. Closed during winter. Deluxe.

GETTING THERE

Nantucket Island is served by ferry from Massachusetts mainland and by air from various points. For car/passenger ferry reservations, contact Steamship Authority at (508) 540-2022. Hy-Line, which provides swifter, passenger-only ferry transport, can be reached by calling (508) 778-2600. Beach club will arrange transportation from Nantucket ferry dock and airport.

CLIFFSIDE BEACH CLUB

The contemporary accommodations of Cliffside Beach Club strike quite a contrast to the older, more traditional bed-and-breakfast inns we passed on the way to the beach. This is Nantucket at its most indulgent.

Set right on the sand facing the Atlantic, Cliffside is the island's only exclusive beach resort. If water, sand, and sun fire your romantic notions, you've come to the right place.

New England old-timers might recall when this was an exclusive members-only resort, where marked and reserved spaces on the sand had everything to do with social standing and tradition. While still a private club, the property has lost its 1950s and 1960s stuffiness; nonmember guests are now warmly welcomed and comfortably accommodated in new and refurbished units ranging from hotel rooms and studios to spacious cottages.

Our springtime visit to Nantucket coincided with an unusual several-weeks-long warm spell, and the beach club, bathed in golden sunshine, was in its glory. There being precious few vacancies, we were able to tour only a couple of units, but what we saw was impressive.

Cliffside Beach Club
P.O. Box 449
Nantucket, MA 02554
Telephone: (508) 228-0618
Web site: www.cliffsidebeachclub.com

ROOMS FOR ROMANCE

Accommodations at Cliffside are situated against the busier main beach or the quieter Gold Coast section of beach on the east side. High-season rates (late June through Labor Day weekend) run from the low $600 range for a hotel-type room to the $1,000 range for a cottage.

The exteriors are typical Nantucket: weathered shingles and white trim. Step inside and you'll be greeted by contemporary freshness and amenities, including fine woodwork by local artisans. Wainscoting figures prominently in the interior design, and beds are contained in matching angled wood frames.

One of the favorite choices among romantics, Room 205, is actually one of the resort's least expensive, fetching rates in the mid $400 range, depending on the season. This unit, classified as a hotel room, has an angled water view.

Other popular romantic accommodations are beachfront studios 201 through 204 and deck rooms 122 through 127. All are offered in the low $600 range, depending on time of year.

Most rooms have queen-sized beds. Cottage 210 has a fireplace. Rooms 206, 207, and 208 do not have water views.

It may be one of our most expensive featured hideaways, but Cliffside Beach Club isn't necessarily out of the reach of economically minded romantics; rates are vastly lower outside high season.

DAYTIME DIVERSIONS

The romance of a nineteenth-century coastal village is preserved at Mystic Seaport, one of New England's most popular attractions. Mystic Aquarium and Institute of Exploration are also popular destinations.

The scenic roads of wonderful LITCHFIELD HILLS will transport you past rural farms and quaint villages to antique stores, galleries, and romantic outdoor places.

From the old stone tower on Haystack Mountain near NORFOLK, you can see the Berkshires and all the way to Long Island Sound.

The Boulders has private lake access as well as Ping-Pong, free rental boats, and windsurfing boards. Nearby NEW PRESTON is a tiny village with a handful of interesting shops.

TABLES FOR TWO

The Boulders and The Mayflower Inn, which are described in this section, have their own highly rated dining rooms. Our innkeepers also recommend:

OLD INN ON THE GREEN, New Marlborough, MA (Norfolk area)
WEST STREET GRILL, Litchfield, CT (Norfolk area)
THE BOAT HOUSE, Lakeville, CT (Norfolk area)

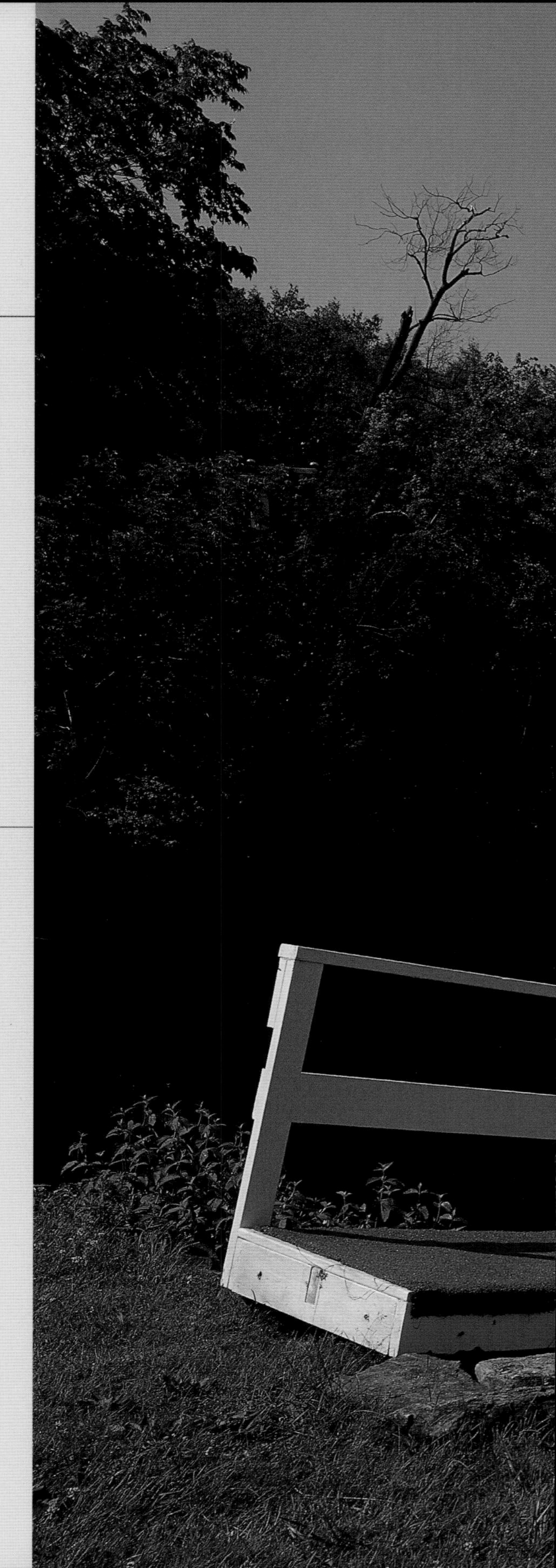

CONNECTICUT

Manor House
69 Maple Avenue
Norfolk, CT 06058
Telephone: (860) 542-5690;
toll-free: (866) 542-5690
Web site: www.manorhouse-norfolk.com

THE FACTS

Nine rooms, each with private bath; two with woodburning fireplaces. Complimentary full breakfast served at small tables or delivered at extra charge to your room. Spa services. Bicycles. No disabled access. Two-night minimum stay required during weekends and holiday periods. Moderate to expensive.

GETTING THERE

From Boston, exit the Massachusetts Turnpike (Interstate 90) at Route 7 and drive south. At Canaan, take Route 44 east to Norfolk. Turn left on Maple Avenue and follow to inn on left. From New York, follow Interstate 84 to Route 8 north at Waterbury, CT. At terminus of highway (Winstead), take Route 44 west and follow to Norfolk. Turn right on Maple Avenue and follow to inn on left.

MANOR HOUSE

Like crunching leaves on an autumn stroll, a soft breeze on a summer night, or a warming fire during a snowfall, Manor House adds just the right touch to a romantic weekend away.

One of our favorite New England destinations, this nine-room property strikes an engaging balance between a tiny bed-and-breakfast inn and a small hotel. Sporting a fairytale Bavarian Tudor façade, the mansion was exquisitely crafted just before the turn of the twentieth century by Charles Spofford, the architect of London's subway system. The artful stained-glass windows that still illuminate the public areas were a housewarming gift from famed glass craftsman Louis Comfort Tiffany.

ROOMS FOR ROMANCE

Don't worry about being assigned a room off the kitchen or parlor; all of the antique-furnished guest quarters are tucked privately away on the second and third floors. One of the most romantic is the English Room (mid $200 range), a bright corner on the second floor with a king-sized four-poster bed and the most sumptuous bathroom in the house. Its centerpiece is a two-person spa tub set against windows and under a ceiling fan. The sink is fitted into an antique dresser.

You may never want to venture out of the very romantic Victorian Room (mid $200 range), a third-floor space whose luscious spa tub for two sits near the foot of a king-sized sleigh bed under a skylight. There's also a fireplace and a sitting area with a pair of wing chairs. The sink is in the room, and the toilet is housed in its own tiny private space.

The beautifully windowed Spofford Room (mid $200 range) holds a handsome period fireplace, a sitting area, and a king-sized bed. The bathroom has a shower, and guests here enjoy a private backyard-view balcony.

Another of our most highly recommended hideaways is the third-floor Country French Room (low $200 range). Featuring a coffered ceiling, tasteful wallpaper, and an exquisite antique carved French bed, the room overlooks the inn's backyard. The tiled bath, which holds a large soaking tub for two, is paneled in cedar and lit by a skylight.

The inn's most private room is the third-floor Chalet Suite (mid $200 range), reached by a private stairway. Situated under the eaves, the suite has a bedroom with a beautiful queen-sized French bed, and a sitting area with a day bed. There's a shower stall under a skylight in the suite's tiny bathroom.

Commanding a very competitive rate in the high $100 range, the cozy La Chambre has a queen-sized brass-and-iron bed, two wing chairs, and a windowed bathroom with a clawfoot-tub-and-shower combination that's original to the house.

The Mayflower Inn
Route 47
Washington, CT 06793
Telephone: (203) 868-9466
Web site: www.mayflowerinn.com

THE FACTS

Twenty-four rooms and suites, each with private bath and plasma television. Heated swimming pool. Tennis court. Spa and fitness facilities. Putting green. Restaurant and lounge. Disabled access. Smoking is discouraged in guest rooms. Two-night minimum stay required during weekends; three-night minimum during holiday periods. Deluxe.

GETTING THERE

From Boston, take Massachusetts Turnpike (Interstate 90) to Interstate 84; take 84 west to Southbury (exit 15). Turn right on Route 6 east and drive five miles to traffic light and Route 47 road sign. Turn left and follow Route 47 for eight miles to Washington. Directions from New York City (a two-hour drive) are available on Web site.

THE MAYFLOWER INN

After sitting closed and neglected for many years, this private school-turned-inn transcended its original luster in the early 1990s through some serious attention by Adriana and Robert Mnuchin. The couple imported European antiques, created spacious marbled bathrooms, installed intimate canopied beds, and restored more than two dozen luscious acres to create a radiant lovers' sanctuary. This is quite possibly southern New England's loveliest inn.

Since our last visit, the inn has added a large destination spa with an indoor swimming pool. New rooms and suites were also planned.

ROOMS FOR ROMANCE

We're hard-pressed to choose between the inn's three separate buildings, known as Mayflower, Speedwell, and Standish. In each, the rooms are elegant, very tastefully furnished, and romantic. The beds are lavishly dressed, and many accommodations have spacious, well-furnished sitting areas or rooms.

The stunning main house, called Mayflower, holds fifteen rooms and suites as well as the inn's dining room. We were impressed with Room 27 (low to mid $400 range) on the second floor, from which guests have pretty views of gardens and lawn. Furnishings include a king-sized canopied bed, an armoire with a television, and a writing desk. The bathroom holds a deep tub for two and a separate shower stall. This is among the Mayflower's least expensive accommodations.

In the Speedwell building, Room 10 features a private balcony in addition to an elegant king-sized canopied bed, a fireplace, and a romantic sitting area. Room 15 is a cozy suite under the eaves, with a large balcony, a full living room, a fireplace, a bedroom with a large window, and a spa tub for two.

Room 26 is a delightful corner room with an enchanting king-sized canopied bed, a chaise, a chair, an armoire, and a fireplace.

At the time of our visit, the Mayflower Inn posted a generous and romantically sensitive check-out time of 1 p.m. Tariffs range from $400 to $600 for rooms; suites range from the mid $600 range to well over $1,000 per night.

Steamboat Inn
73 Steamboat Wharf
Mystic, CT 06355
Telephone: (860) 536-8300
Web site: www.steamboatinnmystic.com

THE FACTS

Ten rooms, each with private bath; six with fireplaces; five with tubs for two. Complimentary continental breakfast served at tables for two or four. Disabled access. Smoking is not permitted. Two-night minimum stay required during weekends. Moderate to deluxe.

GETTING THERE

From Interstate 95 northbound, take exit 89 and turn right off exit. Continue to Route 1 and turn left. From Route 1, turn right on Water Street and left into gated parking lot. Proceed left and follow driveway to end.

STEAMBOAT INN

Don't be put off by the anonymous entrance from a public parking lot. The real mystique of Mystic unfolds once inside your romantic guest room.

Occupying a coveted village spot along the Mystic River just off Main Street, Steamboat Inn is a modern two-story hostelry with large, generously windowed, stylishly decorated rooms along with luxurious bathrooms. Half of the rooms have whirlpool tubs for two; six feature woodburning fireplaces.

Despite its central location within walking distance of Mystic attractions, restaurants, and boutiques, the inn offers surprising peace and quiet, even during the bustling daytime hours. Evenings often find guests curled up by their guest-room windows, watching the parade of pleasure boats pass by only a few yards away.

In the morning, breakfast is served informally from the bar of a second-floor common room with a black-and-white checkerboard floor. Guests dine at tables for two or four.

ROOMS FOR ROMANCE

Guest rooms feature unusual angles and each is individually styled; you won't be greeted by standard cookie-cutter arrangements here.

Kathleen (around $300), the room we stayed in, is a spacious abode with a king-sized canopied bed. French doors open to a separate sitting room with a couch, a chair, and an armoire that conceals a television. The wainscoted bathroom holds a spa tub for two and a separate shower stall. Look out the window and you may see a yacht or sailboat at anchor.

Another top romantic choice is Carolyn (around $300), a nicely windowed and more private room that offers a sitting area, a hidden kitchenette, and a spa tub for two.

Ariadne (high $200 range) is the inn's designated honeymoon room. Located on the second floor, it boasts a sweeping harbor view, a canopied bed, a love seat facing a fireplace, and a spa tub for two in the bathroom. Ariadne is the only second-floor room with a spa tub for two.

Similarly priced is Mystic, a second-floor corner with wraparound windows. A view of the fireplace and harbor is offered from the four-poster bed. The small bathroom holds an individual-sized whirlpool-bath-and-shower combination. The Annie Wilcox room (mid $200 range) has a king-sized bed and a single-sized spa tub.

We didn't find an undesirable guest chamber in the inn, but because of occasional foot traffic along a harbor walk that runs past the downstairs windows, couples in these rooms will need to draw the drapes and sacrifice the river view in order to ensure complete privacy. For this reason, we prefer the inn's upstairs rooms, where a private harbor view will surely enhance your intimate experiences.

DAYTIME DIVERSIONS

More than a half-dozen fabulous mansions from NEWPORT's Gilded Age are open for public tours. If time permits a visit to only one, we recommend the Breakers, summer home of the Cornelius Vanderbilt family. The estate is on Ochre Point Avenue, just blocks from Cliffside Inn. Visit www.newportmansions.org for more information.

On a sunny day, the Cliff Walk, which winds along the rocky Atlantic past Newport's grand estates, is a romantic must. Hammersmith Farm, the summer White House during the Kennedy administration, is also open for guided tours.

The International Tennis Hall of Fame is on Bellevue Avenue in NEWPORT, and the Museum of Yachting is located in FORT ADAMS STATE PARK.

TABLES FOR TWO

PUERINI'S, Newport
LA PETITE AUBERGE, Newport
WHITE HORSE TAVERN, Newport
THE BLACK PEARL, Newport
SARDELLA'S, Newport

RHODE ISLAND

THE FACTS

Fifty-one rooms, each with private bath. Restaurant, bar, and room service. Heated indoor pool. Spa and sauna. Fitness facility. Billiard room. Massage services. Disabled access. Deluxe.

GETTING THERE

From Boston and points north and east, follow Route 24 south (becomes Route 114) into downtown Newport to end. At traffic light, turn left on Thames Street. Take first left on Mary Street and follow for one block to hotel on right.

VANDERBILT HALL HOTEL

Constructed as the Newport Men's Social Club a century ago, thanks to a donation from the son of Cornelius Vanderbilt, this impressive building actually served most of its life as a YMCA. The foundation of the late heiress Doris Duke purchased the property with an eye to restoration, but instead the building languished. In more recent years, an infusion of $11 million transformed the former social club into a stately hotel.

The hotel is well equipped, boasting comfortable public areas as well as a basement-level indoor swimming pool and even a billiard room. Guests may either venture on foot to numerous nearby Newport restaurants or take advantage of the Vanderbilt Hall Hotel Restaurant and its martini bar. Guests in-the-know head for the rooftop deck to watch the sunsets.

ROOMS FOR ROMANCE

The room décor is as varied as the room categories. While one room might be delicately feminine in style, its neighbor might exude a more traditional flair. Others are inspired by sports and recreation. However, all have first-rate Egyptian linens, down comforters, and comfortable furnishings.

Tariffs begin at around $300; however, some guests have described certain of the hotel's rooms as comparatively small and expensive. Some rooms do not have views, and the upstairs studies found in some rooms, while possibly attractive to business travelers, seem somewhat superfluous for those on a romantic getaway.

For a romantic getaway, we recommend you consider a one-bedroom suite (mid $400 range), with a living area and a bathroom on the lower level and a nice bedroom and bathroom with a spa tub on the upper level. Smaller junior suites are offered in the mid $300 range.

VANDERBILT HALL HOTEL
41 Mary Street
Newport, RI 02840
Telephone: (401) 846-6200;
toll-free: (800) VANHALL
Web site: www.vanderbilthall.com

Adele Turner Inn
93 Pelham Street
Newport, RI 02840
Telephone toll-free: (800) 845-1811
Web site: www.adeleturnerinn.com

THE FACTS

Thirteen rooms, each with private bath and fireplace. Morning coffee, tea, and juice delivered to your room. Complimentary full breakfast served at tables for two. Complimentary afternoon refreshments. Twice-daily maid service. High-speed wireless Internet service in most rooms. Disabled access. Two-night minimum stay required during weekends; three-night minimum stay during select summer, fall, and holiday periods. Expensive to deluxe.

GETTING THERE

From Boston and points north and east, follow Interstate 93 to Route 24 south (becomes Route 114) into Middleton. Turn left at traffic light and follow Route 214 signs for approximately ten minutes to beach area. Cross beach on causeway and follow into Newport along Memorial Boulevard and up hill. Turn right on Bellevue Avenue and turn left on Pelham. Follow to inn on left.

ADELE TURNER INN

The more than two dozen tall, arched windows will be the first things that catch your eye from the street, but the sumptuously romantic rooms will be what lingers in your memory long after a visit to Adele Turner Inn. And since the inn offers a baker's dozen of rooms, each offering a decidedly different experience, you'll likely be back for more again and again.

Reportedly Rhode Island's oldest lodging house still serving guests, the mansion was built in 1855 to provide temporary housing for sea captains and officers in the employ of shipping magnate Augustus Littlefield, whose former home still stands across the street.

The inn is located in the heart of Newport's Historic Hill, on the first gas-lit street in America. Listed on the National Register of Historic Places, the inn is named after Philadelphia socialite Adele Turner, who spent summers in Newport and whose mysterious daughter, Beatrice, is the subject of a collection of haunting self-portraits that hang here and in the former Turner home, now the Cliffside Inn (see separate description, page 118). The Adele Turner and Cliffside Inns are part of the same enterprise, which also operates Newport's Abigail Stoneman Inn.

ROOMS FOR ROMANCE

A world-class romantic retreat reminiscent of Newport's Gilded Age, the Tycoon Suite (mid $500 range) is the inn's largest and finest accommodation. In this opulent suite, a large tub for two sits in its own space between the bedroom and the sitting room with a fireplace.

The Harborview Spa room ($500 range) opens to a private rooftop deck furnished with a spa tub for two, served up with a sweeping vista of the neighborhood, Newport Harbor, and Narragansett Bay.

Movie memorabilia adorn the Great Gatsby Suite (high $400 range), which offers a sitting room with a couch and a fireplace, an alcove with a spa tub for two, and a bedroom holding an ornate queen-sized French bed.

Three of the inn's impressive tall, arched windows belong to the Hall of Fame Room (mid $300 range), which is furnished with a queen-sized sleigh bed and decorated with tennis memorabilia. The bathroom has a tub-and-shower combination.

Some rooms have flat-screen LCD televisions and DVD players. Other rooms have videocassette players and video library access.

THE FACTS

Sixteen rooms, each with private bath and fireplace. Complimentary coffee, tea, and juice delivered to your room. Complimentary full breakfast served in dining room at communal table. Complimentary afternoon tea and refreshments. Twice-daily maid service. No disabled access. Two-night minimum stay required during weekends; two- or three-night minimum during select summer and fall weekends and holiday periods. Expensive to deluxe.

GETTING THERE

From Interstate 195 at Fall River, MA, follow Route 24 south to Route 114 south. Route 114 becomes West Main Road in Newport. Turn left on Valley Road (Route 214) and follow south as Valley Road curves right onto Memorial Boulevard. From Memorial Boulevard, turn left on Cliff Avenue and left on Seaview Avenue to inn on left.

CLIFFSIDE INN
2 Seaview Avenue
Newport, RI 02840
Telephone: (401) 847-1811;
toll-free: (800) 845-1811
Web site: www.cliffsideinn.com

CLIFFSIDE INN

NEWPORT

The many paintings of Beatrice Turner, a beautiful heiress whose family resided long ago in what is now Cliffside Inn, convey a haunting, romantic quality to this eclectic Victorian. Sadly, romance was apparently missing from Beatrice's lonely life. As evidenced by her personal diary and scores of self-portraits, many of which line the stairwell and public rooms, Beatrice was self-obsessed, leading the life of a reclusive artist after the death of her parents.

Built in 1880 as a summer getaway for the governor of Maryland, the mansion passed to the Turner family at the turn of the century. It was in these grand rooms that Beatrice painted more than one thousand portraits of herself and her family. Although much of the artwork was destroyed after Beatrice's death in the late 1940s, the surviving paintings speak volumes about the artist's life, from radiant youth to tragically lonely middle age.

Romance may have eluded the previous owner, but it pervades the Cliffside today. This informal and genial inn is not only an ideal base from which to explore all of Newport's charms, it's a great place to simply cozy up with someone special.

In addition to fabulous bathrooms, Cliffside has other romantic assets, including direct access to Newport's famous Cliff Walk, where the two of you can stroll along the Atlantic past grand mansions from the Gilded Age. Cornelius Vanderbilt's magnificent Breakers and other neighboring estates are open for tours and are just a few blocks from the inn.

ROOMS FOR ROMANCE

Although it's hard to choose favorites, we're drawn to the three large luxury suites in Seaview Cottage (low $600 range), a separate charming New England Cape–styled home that is part of the Cliffside compound. Among these is the Seaview Suite, a world-class honeymoon hideaway that the two of you will find difficult to vacate. The bedroom holds an ornate carved king-sized French bed placed next to a native stone wall with a fireplace. The sitting room has a sofa and another fireplace, while the "bathing suite," one of the most romantic bathrooms in all of New England, shares a fireplace with the sitting room and has an exotic Jacuzzi Allure spa tub equipped with steam bath and shower features as well as video and audio.

Among the inn's other popular rooms is Miss Beatrice's (low to mid $400 range) on the second floor. It's a spacious chamber with a queen-sized bed, a woodburning fireplace, and a bay-window seat. In the bathroom is a spa tub for two set in a bay window and, for your romantic pleasure, a separate shower with dual fixtures.

Another favorite among traveling romantics is the Governor's Suite (mid $500 range), a bright third-floor space equipped with a love seat, a king-sized four-poster bed, and a two-sided fireplace. The fabulous bathroom is a warm-water fantasyland, holding a whirlpool tub as well as a one-of-a-kind antique Victorian "bird cage" shower with a sensual full-body, total-surround spray.

Our night here was spent in the Turner Suite (mid $400 range), also high on the third floor. Its handsome antique queen-sized bed has a half canopy, and the romantic bathroom, with a black-and-white tiled floor, contains a large spa tub for two equipped with a hand-held shower attachment. A separate skylit sitting room, located between the bed and bathroom, holds a love seat, a dressing table, and bookshelves.

THE FACTS

Twenty rooms, each with private bath; six with woodburning fireplaces. Complimentary full breakfast buffet served in dining room at communal table. Complimentary afternoon tea and refreshments. No disabled access. Two-night minimum stay required during weekends from November to May; three-night minimum during weekends from Memorial Day through October. Two- and three-night minimum stays during holiday periods. Expensive to deluxe.

GETTING THERE

From Boston, follow Interstate 93 south to Route 24 south (exit left) via Sakonnet River Bridge. After crossing bridge, take exit 1/Route 138 south to Middletown and Newport Beaches and follow for seven miles to Route 138A (stoplight). Turn left onto Route 138A and follow signs to Newport Beaches. Continue on Route 138A for two miles. At second set of stoplights, turn left. Continue for two miles, past Easton's Beach and up hill, now Memorial Boulevard, to Thames Street. Turn left on Thames Street and turn left onto Brewer Street. Inn parking lot is first right off Brewer Street.

The Francis Malbone House
392 Thames Street
Newport, RI 02840
Telephone: (401) 846-0392;
toll-free: (800) 846-0392
Web site: www.malbone.com

THE FRANCIS MALBONE HOUSE

In Newport, our recommended destinations capture delightfully different moods: quiet, well-established neighborhoods or the lively harbor-village setting of the Francis Malbone House.

Harbor shops and attractions are literally a few steps away from the inn, but the fast pace of the village slows to a pleasant crawl inside this charming Colonial home, built in the mid-1700s for a prominent shipping merchant. The inn was expanded in the mid-1990s and more recently an adjoining structure, the Benjamin Mason House, became part of the property.

Boasting a glistening, cream-colored brick façade, this handsome inn belies its age of over two hundred years. The interior spaces are also fresh and elegant, with several nicely furnished parlors and living rooms providing quiet corners for traveling romantics. A well-tended and comfortable backyard garden, another of the inn's pleasing features, serves as a relaxing haven after a day of combing the bustling village.

ROOMS FOR ROMANCE

The least expensive rooms are the Gardenside accommodations, which are simple and elegant and carry rates in the mid $200 range. Two of these have fireplaces, and all have queen-sized beds. For about $50 more, the two of you will get a peek of Newport Harbor and a fireplace.

For a romantic getaway, we recommend the four Newport rooms (low $300 range), located on the second floor of the courtyard wing. These have king-sized beds, spa tubs, and fireplaces. Some of the first-floor Courtyard rooms have semiprivate courtyards.

The Benjamin Mason Suite (mid $400 range) is a spacious, nicely wallpapered second-floor accommodation furnished with a king-sized bed, a sitting area, a fireplace, a spa tub for two, and a separate shower. Guests here share downstairs parlors with inhabitants of the Stillhouse Room, another nice hideaway.

The inn's new sister property, Hilltop Inn, had not yet opened at the time of our most recent travels. The inn offers five bedrooms with spa tubs, fireplaces, flat-screen televisions, and a fitness facility. Hilltop Inn is located at the corner of Bellevue Avenue and Kay Street.

Index

MORE RESOURCES FOR ROMANTIC TRAVELS

WEEKENDS FOR TWO IN NORTHERN CALIFORNIA: 50 ROMANTIC GETAWAYS
The original romantic travel guide that started it all, now in its fourth edition.

WEEKENDS FOR TWO IN THE WINE COUNTRY: 50 ROMANTIC NORTHERN CALIFORNIA GETAWAYS
Destinations from Mendocino County to the wine country of the Central Coast.

WEEKENDS FOR TWO IN SOUTHERN CALIFORNIA: 50 ROMANTIC GETAWAYS
Intimate destinations from the Santa Barbara coast to the sultry desert, now in its third edition.

WEEKENDS FOR TWO IN THE PACIFIC NORTHWEST: 50 ROMANTIC GETAWAYS
Coastal, mountain, and island hideaways in Oregon, Washington, and British Columbia.

WEEKENDS FOR TWO IN THE SOUTHWEST: 50 ROMANTIC GETAWAYS
Enchanting destinations in Arizona, New Mexico, and the Four Corners Region.

With more than 150 color photographs and hundreds of room descriptions in each book, these are the definitive travel guides to the nation's most romantic destinations. All are authored by Bill Gleeson and published by Chronicle Books. For additional information about these volumes, visit www.billgleeson.com.

CAST YOUR VOTE! NEW ENGLAND'S MOST ROMANTIC HOTEL OR INN

Complete and mail this form to Bill Gleeson, *Weekends for Two,* Chronicle Books, 85 Second Street, Sixth Floor, San Francisco, CA 94105.

Our favorite New England romantic retreat (does not have to be featured in this book):

NAME OF HOTEL/INN: ______________________________

CITY/TOWN: ______________________________

THIS PLACE IS SPECIAL BECAUSE: ______________________________

6
29